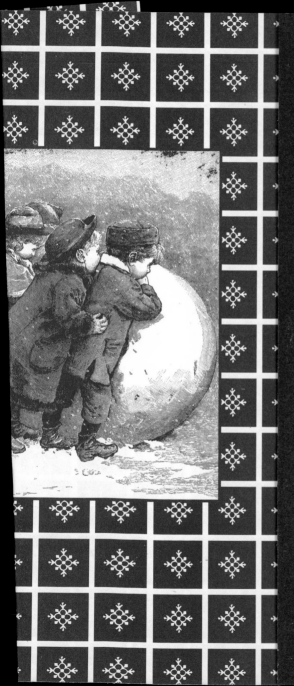

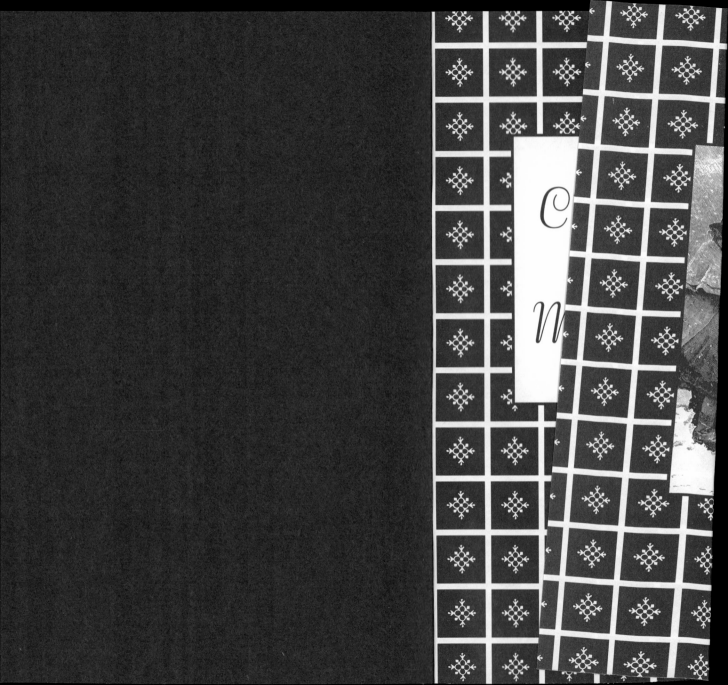

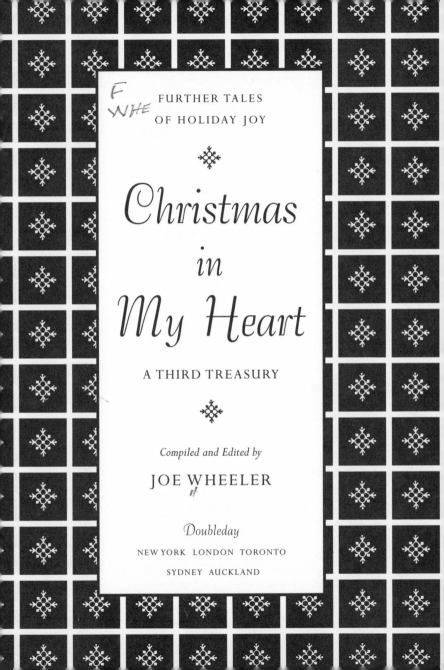

FURTHER TALES
OF HOLIDAY JOY

Christmas in My Heart

A THIRD TREASURY

Compiled and Edited by

JOE WHEELER

Doubleday
NEW YORK LONDON TORONTO
SYDNEY AUCKLAND

PUBLISHED BY DOUBLEDAY
a division of Bantam Doubleday Dell
Publishing Group, Inc.
1540 Broadway, New York, New York 10036

DOUBLEDAY and the portrayal of an anchor with a
dolphin are trademarks of Doubleday, a division of
Bantam Doubleday Dell Publishing Group, Inc.

Book Design by Jennifer Ann Daddio

Woodcut illustrations are from
the library of Joe Wheeler.

Library of Congress Cataloging-in-Publication Data
Christmas in my heart. Selections
Christmas in my heart: a third treasury: further
tales of holiday joy / compiled and edited by
Joe Wheeler. — 1st ed.
p. cm.
Short stories chiefly selected from the volumes of
Christmas in My Heart published by Review and Herald
Pub. Association, c1922–c1996.
1. Christmas stories, American. I. Wheeler, Joe L.,
1936– . II. Title.
PS648.C45C4472 1998
813'.0108334—dc21 98-16727
CIP

ISBN 0-385-49317-7

1 3 5 7 9 10 8 6 4 2

Dedication

Mark J. H. Fretz

Without his enthusiasm, vision, graphics and art expertise, these Christmas treasuries would never have been.

Hence I dedicate the first three *Christmas in My Heart* treasuries to my chief editor, and cherished friend.

$\mathcal{A}$cknowledgments

Introduction: "Snow and Christmas," by Joe Wheeler, Copyright © 1994 (Revised, 1998). Printed by permission of the author.

"The Littlest Orphan and the Christ Baby," by Margaret E. Sangster, Jr. Included in Sangster's collection, *The Littlest Orphan and Other Christmas Stories.* Round Table Press, New York: 1928.

"Unlucky Jim," by Arthur S. Maxwell. Printed by permission of D. Malcolm Maxwell and the Review and Herald® Publishing Association.

"Christmas Echo," by Les Thomas. Published in *The Fort Worth Star-Telegram,* December 25, 1976. Reprinted by permission of *The Fort Worth Star-Telegram.*

"Running Away from Christmas," by Annie Hamilton Donnell. Published in *The Youth's Instructor,* December 26, 1916. Text used by permission of Review and Herald® Publishing Association.

"The Promise of the Doll," by Ruth C. Ikerman. Reprinted by permission of The Christian Herald Association.

"The Fir Tree Cousins," by Lucretia D. Clapp. Published in *The Youth's Instructor,* December 18, 1928. Reprinted by permission of Review and Herald® Publishing Association.

"The Locking In of Lisabeth," by Temple Bailey. If anyone can provide knowledge of earliest publication and date of this old story, please relay this information to Joe L. Wheeler, care of Doubleday Religion Department.

"Have You Seen the Star?" by Margaret Slattery. Reprinted by permission of The Salvation Army and *The War Cry.*

Contents

Snow and Christmas

✦

INTRODUCTION

Snow. Why is it that so many Christmas stories feature it? Why is it that Christmas is somehow perceived as incomplete without it? And . . . with it . . . the longed-for icing on the Christmas cake.

Could it be because in this ever more computerized world we live in, it represents one of Nature's wild cards, its very unpredictability and untameability sources of its attraction?

Could it be because it is such a beautifier? No matter what the object, nothing snow touches can possibly remain ugly—it is magic. Only love beautifies more than snow.

Could it be because it represents renewal, new opportunities to begin again?

Could it be because the arrival of snow once again is a jolting reminder of the swift passage of time (that another year's worth of sand has sifted through the hourglass of life)?

Could it be because it makes us think of skiing, ice-skating, sledding, snowmobiling, sleighing, all the winter sports?

Could it be because the Christmas tree is such an integral part of Christmas? And, of course, few living things are more breathtaking than pines or firs flocked with snow.

Could it be because when we think of Christmas services, concerts, cantatas, oratorios, pageants, midnight services we generally associate them with cold weather, with snow?

Could it be because when snow starts to fall, subconsciously we feel renewed, cleansed—for doesn't the Good Book promise that because of Christ's love and sacrifice, our once scarlet sins are now as white as the snowflakes cascading out of the sky?

Could it be because snow is such an insulator (walling the world out and the family in)? Outside blizzards may rage with blind fury, but so long as those you love are safe inside it is an experience to enjoy, to revel in, to remember through the years. The Janus side of snow is a warm crackling fire in the fireplace; hot cider, chocolate, or wassail.

For it is a time when many of our family memories are made and so many of them have to do with snow:

"Remember the time when we were snowed in for three days?"

"Remember the time when a blizzard knocked out electricity for a week and we spent the entire vacation huddled next to the fireplace?"

"Remember when snow marooned us, so we had to spend Christmas in an airport?"

Each of us can think of such memories—each tied to snow. Could it be that Nordic countries' near monopoly on Christmas stories is a by-product of the snow factor?

With all these questions in mind, I analyzed the first three Christmas collections in order to find out how many of them featured snow. The answer: 24 out of 43 (more than half). Let's take a look at each of our Doubleday *Christmas in My Heart* treasuries and note the stories which feature snow in any way. In each case, ask yourself if you would have liked them as much had snow been excluded.

Of the sixteen stories in the First Treasury, eight are snow-related: In "The Last Straw," the depth of a little boy's hurt is measured by his willingness to spend Christmas alone in the snow rather than face a soured sibling relationship inside. In "A Father for Christmas," the entire story hinges on snow country terminology, wearing apparel, and equipment. In "Christmas in the New World," it is the early snow which makes it impossible to go to town for Christmas presents, and thus is born the willow Christmas. In "Charlie's Blanket," softly falling snow and cold weather result in a child's ultimate gift to the Christ Child. In "A Full House," the contrast between near blizzard conditions outside and the fire-lit haven inside is what gives the story its power. In "My Christmas Miracle," the grim, grayish world of snow mirrors a feeling of abandonment, and the post-storm starlight mirrors reunion with God. In "A Day of Pleasant Bread," snow has transformed the ugly and the plain into a wonderland of beauty, and serves as a vehicle of regeneration. In "Stranger, Come Home," snow both enhances the contrast between East and West and the contrast between sister and sister-in-law. In "The Bells of Christmas Eve," both the snow of New England and the snow of Europe prove to be key ingredients in the story.

Of the fourteen stories in the Second Treasury, eight are snow-related: In "David's Star of Bethlehem," it is snow which provides the desired isolation from Christmas; paradoxically, this very snow brings with it restitution of Christmas, family, and love. In "A Certain Small Shepherd," snow is what—by precluding Christmas, as usual—opens the door of opportunity for a for a Christmas miracle. In "Christmas Is for Families," while snow is not physically present, because a daughter chooses home over snow, it plays a key role in the story even in its absence. In "Jolly Miss Enderby," the setting sun illuminates the snow with a fiery glow to begin the narrative, and the coalescence of snow, church bells, and tears ends it. In "Roses in December," the snow-like white frost stage set for the denouement enhances an unearthly radiance by moonlight. In "Lonely Tree," the protagonist is excessively lonely because one of her coworkers gets to go home to snow and she does not. In "A Few Bars in the Key of G," snow, represented by the 12,000-foot Berthoud Pass, separates knowing from not knowing, love lost from love regained. In "The Snow of Christmas," snow represents coldness, loneliness, and loss in the first part of the story; and restoration of the circle of three in the last part.

Of the thirteen stories in this Third Collection, eight are snow related: In "Christmas Echo," snow is associated

with both early tragedy and eventual healing. In "Running Away from Christmas," while snow is implied throughout, it does not actually appear until the concluding scene. In "The Fir Tree Cousins," the entire focus of the story has to do with the snowy world of the Maine Woods. In "The Locking in of Lisabeth," the snow sifting down between the two buildings represents barriers between generations; and snow on the Judge's coat represents a turning from dark to light, from coldness to warmth. In "Have You Seen the Star?," dream-snow is equated with death of family love. In "On Christmas Day in the Morning," only by struggling through deep snow can the family return home; once there, the warmth within is only enhanced by the cold without. In "Christmas Lost and Found," happiness is lost in snow, and happiness is regained in snow. In " 'Meditation' in a Minor Key," virtually the entire story is set in snow: It is a winter story from start to finish; each of the crucial passages takes place against a back-drop of snow.

THE THIRD COLLECTION

With this third Doubleday collection, I can confirm that these little hardbacks have created their own success story. It is amazing how many devotees are satisfied with nothing

less. Any number of times I've asked myself why. At book signings I watch intently, in search of answers. I believe I now have them.

First of all, there are a lot of people who love small things, miniatures, if you please. These books are no bigger than many paperbacks, so they can be transported easily. They fit on the smallest bookshelves.

Second, they are miniature works of art, pleasing to the eye, and the well-chosen graphics, type-face, and colors contribute to their overall look, making them collectibles.

Third, each season more readers fall in love with the old-fashioned woodcut illustrations, most well over a century old—when the year 2000 A.D. is reached, they will seem *two* centuries old. Every *fin de siècle* creates a wave of nostalgia for the past; the end of a millennium will create a much greater wave. But it is more than nostalgia: The woodcut takes us back to a simpler, kinder, softer world where values were admired and lived by rather than being an object of ridicule by a media. So it is that browsers leaf through the books, delighted to find an old-timey woodcut for each story.

Fourth, while the books may be bought because of the illustrations, they are gathered to the heart because of the stories themselves. For those who have resigned themselves to the conviction that a Christmas story is a Christmas story is a Christmas story, these *Christmas in My Heart* stories prove to be a real shock. Each one of them carries a great cargo of emotional freight; the stories that do not, never make it in! *And,* the stories are Christ-centered rather than Santa Claus–centered, in terms of the values.

It is because of these reasons that I believe the story of these small hardbacks has only just begun.

As to the thirteen stories in this third collection, four of the authors are already developing a following as a result of their inclusion in the earlier collections: Margaret Sangster ("Lonely Tree"), Annie Hamilton Donnell ("Rebecca's Only Way"), and Hartley Dailey ("The Red Mittens") in *Christmas in My Heart 2;* and Temple Bailey ("Candle in the Forest") in *Christmas in My Heart 1.* The other eight authors—excluding me—are likely to be new, but I daresay, not for long. *Especially* such heavy-weight story writers as Arthur Maxwell and Grace Richmond.

Unquestionably, the biggest lateral excitement this year was generated by Dr. James Dobson's decision to return to his personal favorite Christmas story, "The Tiny Foot," by Frederic Loomis *(Christmas in My Heart 2)* for the Focus on the Family Christmas story of the year—over

3,000,000 homes received the story, complete with new illustrations. Amazing, isn't it? The impact just one story can have!

CODA

Virtually every day's mail brings welcome correspondence from you. Many of your letters are testimonials to the power of certain stories; virtually *all* of them express gratitude for the series. Others include favorite stories for possible inclusion down the line (some of them Christmas-related and others tying in with other genre collections we are working on). These letters from you not only brighten each day for us—but they help to provide the stories which make possible future story anthologies.

May the good Lord bless and guide each of you.

You may contact me at the following address:

Joe Wheeler, Ph.D.
C/o Doubleday Religion Department
1540 Broadway
New York, New York 10036

The Littlest Orphan and the Christ Baby

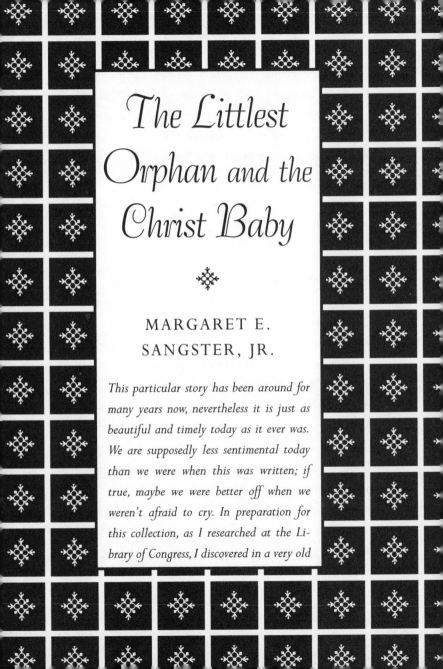

MARGARET E. SANGSTER, JR.

This particular story has been around for many years now, nevertheless it is just as beautiful and timely today as it ever was. We are supposedly less sentimental today than we were when this was written; if true, maybe we were better off when we weren't afraid to cry. In preparation for this collection, as I researched at the Library of Congress, I discovered in a very old collection the original text of the story (significantly different from the eroded version I had always known—and more beautiful).

Margaret Sangster is little known today, but early in this century, she was one of the most loved and appreciated writers and editors of inspirational literature in America.

The Littlest Orphan gazed up into the face of the Christ Baby, who hung, gilt-framed and smiling, above the mantelshelf. The mantel was dark, made of a black, mottled marble that suggested tombstones, and the long room—despite its rows of neat, white beds—gave an impression of darkness, too. But the picture above the mantel sparkled and scintillated and threw off an aura of sheer happiness. Even the neat IN MEMORIAM card tacked to the wall directly under it could not detract from its joy. All of rosy babyhood, all of unspoiled laughter, all of the beginnings of life were in that picture! And the Littlest Orphan sensed it, even though he did not quite understand.

The Matron was coming down the room with many wreaths, perhaps a dozen of them, braceleting her thin arm. The wreaths were just a trifle dusty; their imitation holly leaves spoke plaintively of successive years of hard usage. But it was only two days before Christmas and the wreaths would not show up so badly under artificial light. The board of trustees, coming for the entertainment on Christmas Eve, never arrived until the early winter dusk had settled down. And the wreaths could be laid away, as soon as the holiday was past, for another twelve months.

The Littlest Orphan, staring up at the picture, did not hear the Matron's approaching footsteps. True, the Matron wore rubber heels—but any other orphan in the whole asylum would have heard her. Only the Littlest Orphan, with his thin, sensitive face and his curious fits of absorption, could have ignored her coming. He started painfully as her sharp voice cut into the silence.

"John," she said, and the frost that made such pretty lacework upon the windowpane wrought havoc with her voice, *"John, what are you doing here?"*

The Littlest Orphan answered after the manner of all small boy-children. "Nothin'!" he said.

Standing before him, the Matron—who was a large woman—seemed to tower. "You are not telling the truth, John," she said. "You have no right to be in the dormitory at this hour. Report to Miss Mace, at once"—Miss Mace was the primary teacher—"and tell her that I said you were to write five extra pages in your copybook. *At once!"*

With hanging head, the Littlest Orphan turned away. It seemed terribly unfair, although it was against the rules to spend any but sleeping hours in the dormitory! He was just learning to write, and five pages meant a whole afternoon of cramped fingers and tired eyes. But how could he explain to this grim woman that the Christ Baby fascinated him, charmed him, and comforted him? How could he explain that the Christ Baby's wide eyes had a way of glancing down, almost with understanding, into his own? How could he tell, with the few weak words of his vocabulary, that he loved the Christ Baby whose smile was so tenderly sweet? That he spent much of his time standing, as he stood now, in the shadow of that smile? He trudged away with never a word, down the length of the room, his clumsy shoes making a feeble clatter on the bare boards of the floor. When he was almost at the door, the Matron called after him.

"Don't drag your feet, John!" she commanded. And so he walked the rest of the way on tiptoe. And closed the door very softly after him.

The halls had already been decorated with long streamers of red and green crepe paper that looped along, in a half-hearted fashion, from picture to picture. The stair railing was wound with more of the paper, and the school-room—where Miss Mace sat stiffly behind a broad desk—was vaguely brightened by red cloth poinsettias set here and there at random. But the color of them was not re-flected in the Littlest Orphan's heart, as he delivered his message and received in return a battered copybook.

As he sat at his desk, writing laboriously about the cat who ate the rat and the dog who ran after the cat, he could hear the other orphans playing outside in the courtyard. Al-ways they played from four o'clock—when school was over—until five-thirty, which was suppertime. It was a rule to play from four until five-thirty. They were running and shouting together, but in a stilted way. The Littlest Orphan did not envy them much. They were all older and stronger than he, and their games were sometimes hard to enjoy. He had been the last baby taken before a new ruling, making six years the minimum entrance age, had gone through. And he was only five years old now. Perhaps it was his very littleness that made the Matron more intolerant of him—he pre-sented to her a problem that could not be met in a mass way. His clothing had to be several sizes smaller than the other clothing; his lessons less advanced. And so on.

Drearily he wrote. And listened, between sentences, to the scratching pen of Miss Mace. . . . The dog had caught the cat. And now the man beat the dog. And then it was time to start all over again, back at the place where the cat ate the rat. Two pages, three pages, four pages. . . . Sur-reptitiously the Littlest Orphan moved his fingers, one by one, and wondered that he was still able to move them. Then, working slowly, he finished the last page and handed the copybook back to the teacher. As she studied it, her face softened slightly.

"Why did the Matron punish you, John?" she asked, as if on impulse, as she made a correction in a sentence.

The Littlest Orphan hesitated for a second. And then said: "I shouldn't have been in th' dormitory," he said slowly. "An' I was!"

Again Miss Mace asked a question.

"But what," she queried, "were you doing there? Why weren't you out playing with the other children?"

She didn't comment upon the fault, but the Littlest Orphan knew that she, also, thought the punishment rather severe. Only it isn't policy to criticize a superior's method of discipline. He answered her second question gravely.

"I was lookin' at th' Christ Baby over the mantel," he said.

As if to herself, Miss Mace spoke. "You mean the picture Mrs. Benchly gave in memory of her son," she murmured, "the pastel." And then, "Why were you looking at it—" She hesitated, and the Littlest Orphan didn't know that she had almost said "dear."

Shyly the child spoke, and wistfulness lay across his thin, small face—an unrealized wistfulness. "He looks so

. . . nice," said the Littlest Orphan gently, "like he had a mother, maybe."

Supper that night was brief, and after supper there were carols to practice in the assembly room. The Littlest Orphan, seated at the extreme end of the line, enjoyed the singing. The redheaded boy, who fought so often in the courtyard, had a high, thrilling soprano. Listening to him, as he sang the solo parts, made the Littlest Orphan forget a certain black eye and a nose that had once been swollen and bleeding. Made him forget lonely hours when he had lain uncomforted in his bed as a punishment for quarreling.

The redheaded boy was singing something about "gold and frank-kin-sense and myrrh." The Littlest Orphan told himself that they must be very beautiful things. Gold—the Christ Baby's frame was of gold—but frank-kin-sense and myrrh were unguessed names. Maybe they were flowers— real flowers that smelled pretty, not red cloth ones. He shut his eyes, singing automatically, and imagined what these flowers looked like—the color and shape of their petals, and whether they grew on tall lily stalks or on short pansy stems.

And then the singing was over, and he opened his eyes with a start and realized that the Matron was speaking.

"Before you go to bed," she was saying, "I want you to understand that you must be on your good behavior until after the trustees leave tomorrow evening. You must not make any disorder in the corridors or in the dormitories—they have been especially cleaned and dusted. You must pay strict attention to the singing; the trustees like to hear you sing! They will all be here, even Mrs. Benchly, who has not visited us since her son died. And if one of you misbehaves—"

She stopped abruptly, but her silence was crowded with meaning, and many a child squirmed uncomfortably in his place. It was only after a moment that she spoke again.

"Good night!" she said abruptly.

And the orphans chorused back, "Good night."

Undressing carefully and swiftly, for the dormitory was cold and the lights were dim, the Littlest Orphan wondered about the trustees—and in particular about the Mrs. Benchly who had lost her son. All trustees were ogres to asylum children, but the Littlest Orphan couldn't help feeling that Mrs. Benchly was the least ogre-like of them all. Somehow she was a part of the Christ Baby's picture, and it was a part of her. If she were responsible for it, she could not be all bad! So ruminating, the Littlest Orphan said his brief prayers—any child who forgot his prayers was punished severely—and slid between the sheets into his bed.

Some of the orphans made a big lump under their bedcovers. The redheaded boy was stocky, and so were others. Some of them were almost fat. But the Littlest Orphan made hardly any lump at all. The sheet, the cotton blanket, and the spread went over him with scarcely a ripple. Often the Littlest Orphan had wished that there might be another small boy who could share his bed. He took up such a tiny section of it. Another small boy would have made the bed seem warmer, somehow, and less lonely. Once two orphans had come to the asylum who were brothers. They had shared things—beds and desks and books. Maybe brothers were unusual gifts from a surprisingly blind providence, gifts that were granted only once in a hundred years! More rare, even, than mothers.

Mothers. The sound of the word had a strange effect upon the Littlest Orphan, even when he said it silently in his soul. It meant so much that he did not comprehend— so much for which he vaguely hungered. Mothers stood for warm arms, and kisses, and soft words. Mothers meant punishments, too, but gentle punishment that did not really come from way inside.

Often the Littlest Orphan had heard the rest talking stealthily about mothers. Some of them could actually remember having owned one! But the Littlest Orphan could not remember. He had arrived at the asylum as a baby— delicate and frail and too young for memories that would later come to bless him and to cause a strange, sharp sort of hurt. When the rest spoke of bedtime stories, and lullabies, and sugar cookies, he listened—wide-eyed and half incredulous—to their halting sentences.

It was growing very cold in the dormitory, and it was dark. Even the faint flicker of light had been taken away. The Littlest Orphan wiggled his toes under the cotton blanket, and wished that sleep would come. Some nights it came quickly, but this night . . . perhaps he was overtired, and it was so cold!

As a matter of habit his eyes searched through the dark for the place where the Christ Baby hung. He could not distinguish even the dim outlines of the gilt frame, but he knew that the Christ Baby was rosy and chubby and smiling, that his eyes were deeply blue and filled with cheer. Involuntarily the Littlest Orphan stretched out his thin hands and dropped them back again against the spread. All about him the darkness lay like a smothering coat, and the Christ Baby, even though he smiled, was invisible. The other children were sleeping. All up and down the long room sounded their regular breathing, but the Littlest Orphan could not sleep. He wanted something that he was unable to define— wanted it with such a burning intensity that the tears crowded into his eyes. He sat up abruptly in his bed—a small, shivering figure with quivering lips and a baby ache in his soul that had never really known babyhood.

Loneliness. It swept about him. More disheartening than the cold. More enveloping than the darkness. There was no fear in him of the shadows in the corner, of the creaking shutters and the narrow stair. Such fears are discouraged early in children who live by rule and routine. No. It was a feeling more poignant than fear, a feeling that clutched at him and squeezed his small body until it was dry and shaking and void of expression.

Of all the children sleeping in the dormitory, the Littlest Orphan was the only child who knew the ache of such loneliness. Even the ones who had been torn away from family ties had, each one of them, something beautiful to keep preciously close. But the Littlest Orphan had nothing—nothing. . . . The loneliness filled him with a strange impulse, an impulse that sent him sliding over the edge of his bed with small arms outflung.

All at once he was crossing the floor on bare, mouse-quiet feet. Past the placidly sleeping children, past the row of lockers, past the table with its neat cloth and black-bound, impressive guest book. Past everything until he stood, a white spot in the blackness, directly under the mantel. The Christ Baby hung above him. And, though the Littlest Orphan could not see, he felt that the blue eyes were looking down tenderly. All at once he wanted to touch the Christ Baby, to hold him tight, to feel the sweetness and warmth of him. Tensely, still moved by the curious impulse, he tiptoed back to where the table stood. Carefully he laid the guest book on the floor; carefully he removed the white cloth. And then staggering under what was to him a great weight, he carried the table noiselessly back with him. Though it was really a small, light table, the Littlest Orphan breathed hard as he set it down. He had to rest, panting for a moment, before he could climb up on it.

All over the room lay silence, broken only by the sleepy sounds of the children. The Littlest Orphan listened almost prayerfully as he clambered up on the tabletop and drew himself to an erect position. His small hands groped along the mantelshelf, touched the lower edge of the gilt frame. But the Christ Baby was still out of reach.

Feverishly, obsessed with one idea, the Littlest Orphan raised himself on tiptoe. His hands gripped the chill marble of the mantel. Tugging, twisting—all with the utmost quiet—he pulled himself up until he was kneeling upon the mantelshelf. Quivering with nervousness as well as the now intense cold, he finally stood erect. And then—only then—he was able to feel the wire and nail that held the Christ Baby's frame against the wall. His numb fingers loosened the wire carefully. And then at last the picture was in his arms.

It was heavy, the picture. And hard. Not soft and warm as he had somehow expected it to be. But it was the Christ Baby nevertheless. Holding it close, the Littlest Orphan fell to speculating upon the ways of getting down, now that both of his hands were occupied. It would be hard to slide from the mantel to the table, and from table to floor, with neither sound nor mishap.

His eyes troubled, his mouth a wavering line in his pinched face, the Littlest Orphan crowded back against the wall. The darkness held now the vague menace of depth. Destruction lurked in a single misstep. It had been a long way up. It would be even longer going down. And he now had the Christ Baby, as well as himself, to care for.

Gingerly he advanced one foot over the edge of the mantel—and drew it back. Sharply. He almost screamed in sudden terror. It was as if the dark had reached out long, bony fingers to pull him from his place of safety. He wanted to raise his hands to his face, but he could not release his hold upon the gilt frame. All at once he realized that his hands were growing numb with the cold and that his feet were numb, too.

The minutes dragged by. Somewhere a clock struck many times. The Littlest Orphan had never heard the clock strike so many times at night before. He cowered back until it seemed to his scared, small mind that he would sink into the wall. And then, as the clock ceased striking, he heard another sound—a sound that brought dread to his heart. It was a step in the hall, a heavy, firm step that—despite rubber heels—was now clearly recognizable. It would be the Matron, making her rounds of the building before she went to bed. As the steps came nearer along the hall, a light, soft and yellow, seemed to grow in the place. It would be the lamp that she carried in her hand.

The Matron reached the door and peered in. And then, with lamp held high, she entered the room. And her swift glance swept the row of white beds—each, but one, with its sleeping occupant.

The Littlest Orphan, on the mantel, clutched the Christ Baby closer in his arms. And waited. It seemed to him that his shivering must shake the room. He gritted his teeth convulsively, as the Matron's eyes found his tumbled, empty bed.

Hastily, forgetting to be quiet, the woman crossed the room. She pulled back the spread, the blanket. And then—

24

❖

as if drawn by a magnet—her eyes lifted and traveled across the room. And found the small, white figure that pressed back into the narrow space. Her voice was sharper even than her eyes, when she spoke.

"John," she called abruptly—and her anger made her forget to be quiet—*"What are you doing up there?"*

Across the top of the Christ Baby's gilt frame, the eyes of the Littlest Orphan stared into the eyes of the Matron with something of the fascination that one sees in the eyes of a bird charmed by a cat or a snake. In narrow, white beds, all over the room, children were stirring, pulling themselves erect, staring. One child snickered behind a sheltering hand. But the Littlest Orphan was conscious only of the Matron. He waited for her to speak again. In a moment she did.

"John," she said, and her voice was burning, and yet chill, with rage, "you are a bad boy. *Come down at once!"*

His eyes blank with sheer fright, his arms clasping the picture close, the Littlest Orphan answered the tone of that voice. With quivering lips he advanced one foot, then the other. And stepped into the space that was the room below. He was conscious that some child screamed. He, himself, did not utter a sound. The Matron started forward. And then he struck the table and rolled with it, and the Christ Baby's splintering picture, into the darkness.

25

The Littlest Orphan spent the next day in bed, with an aching head and a wounded heart. The pain of his bruises did not make a great difference; neither did the threats of the Matron penetrate his consciousness. Only the bare space over the mantel mattered—only the blur of blue and yellow and red upon the hearth, where the pastel had struck. Only the knowledge that the Christ Baby—the meaning of all light and happiness—was no more, troubled him.

There was a pleasant stir about the asylum. An excited child, creeping into the dormitory, told the Littlest Orphan that one of the trustees had sent a tree. And that another was donating ice cream. And that there were going to be presents. But the Littlest Orphan did not even smile. His wan face was set and drawn. Dire punishment waited him after his hurts were healed. And there would be no Christ Baby to go to for comfort and cheer when the punishment was over.

The morning dragged on. Miss Mace brought his luncheon of bread and milk and was as kind to him as she dared to be—your Miss Maces have been made timorous by a too forceful world. Once, during the early afternoon, the Matron came in to examine his bruised head, and once a maid came to rub the colored stains from the hearth. The Littlest Orphan caught his breath as he watched her. And then it began to grow dark, and the children were brought upstairs to be washed and dressed in clean blouses for the entertainment. They had been warned not to talk with him, and they obeyed, for there were folk watching and listening. But even so, flickers of conversation—excited, small-boy conversation— drifted to the Littlest Orphan's waiting ears. Someone had said there was to be a Santa Claus. In a red suit and a white beard. Perhaps it was true. The Littlest Orphan slid down under the covers and pulled the sheet high over his aching head. He didn't want the rest to know that he was crying.

The face-washing was accomplished swiftly. Just as swiftly were the blouses adjusted to the last tie, string, and button. And then the children filed downstairs, and the Littlest Orphan was left alone again. He pulled himself up gingerly until he sat erect, and buried his face in his hands.

Suddenly, from downstairs, came the sound of music. First, the tiny piano, and then the voices of the children as they sang. Automatically the Littlest Orphan joined in, his voice quavering weakly through the empty place. He didn't want to sing—there was neither rhythm nor melody in his heart. But he had been taught to sing those songs, and sing them he must.

First there was "O Little Town of Bethlehem." And then a carol. And then the one about "Gold and frank-kin-sense and myrrh." Strange that the words did not mean flowers tonight! And then there was a hush—perhaps it was a prayer. And then a burst of clapping and a jumble of glad cries. Perhaps that was the Santa Claus in his trappings of white and scarlet. The Littlest Orphan's tears came like hot rain to his tired eyes.

There was a sound in the hall. A rubber-heeled step upon the bare floor. The Littlest Orphan slid down again under the covers, until only the bandage on the brow was at all visible. When the Matron stooped over him, she could not even glimpse his eyes. With a vigorous hand she jerked aside the covers.

"Sick or not," she told him, "you've got to come downstairs. Mrs. Benchly wants to see the boy who broke her son's memorial picture. I'll help you with your clothes."

Trembling violently, the Littlest Orphan allowed himself to be wedged into undies and a blouse and a pair of coarse, dark trousers. He laced his shoes with fingers that shook with mingled fear and weakness. And then he followed the Matron out of the dormitory and through the long halls, with their mocking festoons of red and green crepe paper, and into the assembly room where the lights were blinding and the Christmas tree was a blaze of glory.

The trustees sat at one end of the room, the far end. They were a mass of dark colors, blacks and browns and somber grays. Following in the wake of the Matron, the Littlest Orphan stumbled toward them. Mrs. Benchly. Would she beat him in front of all the rest? Would she leap at him accusingly from that dark mass? He felt smaller than he had ever felt before, and more inadequate.

The children were beginning to sing again. But despite their singing, the Matron spoke. Not loudly, as she did to the children, but with a curious deference.

"This is John, Mrs. Benchly," she said, "the child who broke the picture."

Biting his lips, so that he would not cry out, the Littlest Orphan stood in the vast shadow of the Matron. He shut his eyes. Perhaps if this Mrs. Benchly meant to strike him, it would be best to have his eyes shut. And then suddenly a voice came, a voice so soft that somehow he could almost feel the velvet texture of it.

"Poor child," said the voice, "he's frightened. And ill, too. Come here, John. I won't hurt you, dear."

Opening his eyes incredulously, the Littlest Orphan stared past the Matron into the sort of face small children dream about. Violet-eyed and tender. Lined, perhaps, and sad about the mouth, and wistful. But so sweet! Graying hair, with a bit of a wave in it, brushed back from a broad, white brow. And slim, white, reaching hands. The Littlest Orphan went forward without hesitation. Something about this lady was reminiscent of the Christ Baby. As her white hand touched his, tightened on it, he looked up into her face with the ghost of a smile.

The children had crowded almost informally to the other end of the room, toward the tree. The dark mass of the trustees was dissolving, breaking up into fragments that followed the children. One of the trustees laughed aloud. Not at all like an ogre. A sudden sense of gladness began, for no understandable reason, to steal across the Littlest Orphan's consciousness. Rudely the voice of the Matron broke in upon it.

"I had warned the children," she said, "not to disturb anything. Last evening, before they retired. John deliberately disobeyed. And the picture is ruined in consequence. What do you think we had better do about it, Mrs. Benchly?"

For a moment the lady with the dream face did not speak. She was drawing the Littlest Orphan nearer, until he touched the satin folds of her black gown. And despite the Matron's voice, he was not afraid. When at last she answered the Matron, he did not flinch.

"I think," she said gently, "that I'll ask you to leave us. I would like to talk with John—alone."

And, as the Matron walked stiffly away, down the length of the room, she lifted the Littlest Orphan into her lap.

"I know," she said, and her voice was even gentler than it had been, "that you didn't mean to break the picture. Did you, dear?"

Eagerly the Littlest Orphan answered, "Oh, no, ma'am!" he told her. I didn't mean t' break th' Christ Baby."

The woman's arms were about him. They tightened suddenly. "You're so young," she said. "You're such a mite of a thing. I doubt if you could understand why I had the picture made. Why I gave it to the home here, to be hung in the dormitory. . . . My little son was all I had after my husband died. And his nursery—it was such a pretty room— had a Christ Child picture on the wall. And my boy always loved the picture. . . . And so when he . . . left . . ."— her voice faltered—"I had an artist copy it. I—I couldn't part with the original! And I sent it to a place where there would be many small boys, who could enjoy it as my son had always . . ." Her voice broke.

The Littlest Orphan stared in surprise at the lady's face. Her violet eyes were misted like April blossoms with the dew upon them. Her lips quivered. Could it be that she, too, was lonesome and afraid? His hand crept up until it touched her soft cheek.

"I *loved* th' Christ Baby," he said simply.

31

The lady looked at him. With an effort she downed the quaver in her voice. "I can't believe," she said at last, "that you destroyed the picture purposely. No matter what she"—her glance rested upon the Matron's stiff figure, half a room away—"may think! John, dear, did you mean to spoil the gift I gave in my small boy's name? Oh, I'm sure you didn't."

All day long the Littlest Orphan had lived in fear and agony of soul. All day long he had known pain—physical pain and the pain of suspense. Suddenly he buried his face in the lady's neck—he had never known before that there was a place in ladies' necks, just made for tiny heads—and the tears came.

Choked by sobs, he spoke. "No'm," he sobbed, "I didn't mean to. . . . It was only because I was cold. And lonesome. An' th' bed was big. An' all th' rest was asleep. An' the Christ Baby always looked so pink . . . an' glad . . . an' warm. An' I wanted t' take him inter my bed. An' cuddle close"—he burrowed his head deeper into the neck—"so that I wouldn't be cold anymore. Or lonesome anymore."

The lady's arms tightened about the Littlest Orphan's body until the pressure almost hurt—but it was a nice sort of hurt. It shocked her, somehow, to feel the thinness of that body. And her tears fell quite unrestrained upon the

Littlest Orphan's bandaged head. And then all at once she bent over. And her lips pressed, ever so tenderly, upon the place where his cheek almost met her ear.

"Not to be cold," she whispered, more to herself than to the Littlest Orphan, "or lonesome anymore! To have the nursery opened again—and the sound of the tiny feet in the empty rooms. To have the Christ Child smiling down upon a sleeping little boy. To kiss bruises away again. . . . Not to be lonesome anymore, or cold—"

Suddenly she tilted back the Littlest Orphan's head; was looking deep, deep into his bewildered eyes.

"John," she said, and his name sounded so different when she said it, "how would you like to come away from here and live in my house, with me? How would you like to be my boy?"

A silence had crept over the other end of the room. One of the trustees, who wore a clerical collar, had mounted the platform. He was reading from the Bible that visiting ministers read from of a Sunday. His voice rang—resonant and rich as an organ tone—through the room.

" 'For unto us a child is born,' " he read, " 'unto us a son is given.' "

The Littlest Orphan, with a sigh of utter happiness, crowded closer into the arms that held him.

And it was Christmas Eve!

Unlucky Jim

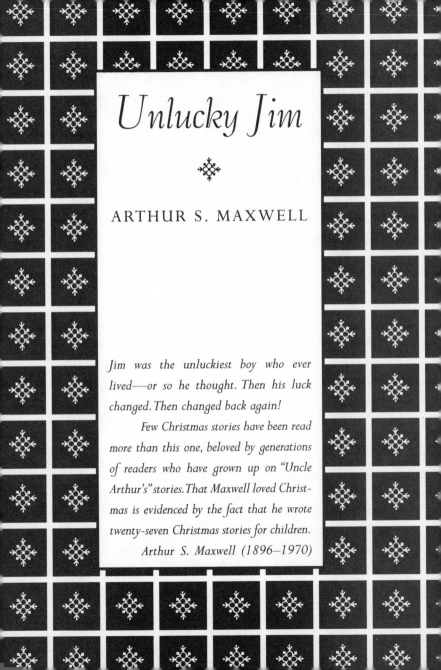

ARTHUR S. MAXWELL

Jim was the unluckiest boy who ever lived—or so he thought. Then his luck changed. Then changed back again!

Few Christmas stories have been read more than this one, beloved by generations of readers who have grown up on "Uncle Arthur's" stories. That Maxwell loved Christmas is evidenced by the fact that he wrote twenty-seven Christmas stories for children.

Arthur S. Maxwell (1896–1970)

lived the first forty years of his life in England and the last thirty-four in America, although he never gave up his British citizenship. For sixteen years, he edited Present Truth in England, and served as editor of Signs of the Times in America for his last thirty-four years.

One of the most prolific writers of his time, altogether he wrote 112 books (seventy-nine for children and thirty-three for adults). They have been published in thirty-three countries and in thirty-seven different languages. Early in his career, he began to publish value-oriented stories for children, each one based on a true incident. As a result of the escalating demand, each year for forty-eight consecutive years a volume of Uncle Arthur's Bedtime Stories was published, with total sales of nearly 44 million copies. His other continuing best seller, The Bible Story, has sold to date about 27 million copies. All told, Maxwell's books have sold a mind-boggling 80 million copies!

Jim thought he was the most unlucky boy that ever had been born. Everything seemed to go wrong with him. His outlook on life was particularly dark just now, for only a few minutes ago his one and only glass marble had rolled down a drain.

But quite apart from this calamity, he had much to make him feel blue. For one thing, he was shivering with cold. He should have had warm stockings and underclothes to wear, but he hadn't any, because there was not enough money to buy them. Father was out of work.

For another thing, he was hungry. It was some hours since lunch, and the bread and butter he had had then seemed to have gone clear down to the South Pole. As he trudged along the streets with his hands in his pockets, he saw lots of other boys and girls going into beautiful homes for their supper, and he knew that he would have to climb up the dirty, narrow stairs of an East End tenement for the little bit of bread and jam that he would get, for there was never enough.

Just then he passed a toy shop, all ablaze with lights and full of everything that might make a boy's heart glad. He stopped a moment and watched other boys and girls coming out with brown paper parcels under their arms. Jim jabbed his hand a little deeper down into his pocket and fingered his penny once again, his very last coin. How he wished that he could buy something to take to his little sister, lying at home so sick—something she would really like.

"If I ain't the unluckiest feller that ever lived!" he said to himself.

But the next day his luck seemed to change. He was walking down the street near his home when a well-dressed lady stopped him.

"Is your name Jimmie Mackay?" she asked.

"Yes, m'm," said Jimmie, surprised, and wondering what was going to happen.

"Well," said the lady, "we have your name on a list at our church, and we want you to come to a special Christmas party next week. Here is a ticket for you."

"Oh, my!" said Jimmie, not knowing what else to say. "But what about Jean—she's my sister, y' know; she'll be better by then, perhaps; she ought to come too."

"I'm afraid we can take only one from each family this time," said the lady kindly. "We will try to take Jean next time."

"Well, that's lucky and unlucky," said Jim to himself as the lady walked away. "Lucky for me and unlucky for poor Jean."

Then a bright idea occurred to him—perhaps he could let Jean go instead of him. He looked at his card. It read: ADMIT BEARER—JIMMIE MACKAY—ONLY.

"Unlucky again!" murmured Jimmie.

So Jimmie went to the party. For the greater part of

38

the time he forgot all about his troubles. Everything was so different, so very wonderful. He had never had so much to eat in all his life.

After supper they all played games until it was time for the presents on the Christmas tree to be given away. What excitement there was then, especially as each child was to be allowed to choose just what he wanted most.

Jim could hardly sit still as he watched the other children going up in front of him. He felt as though he were on pins and needles. He had seen such a wonderful toy fire engine hanging on the tree—something he had wanted all his life—and how he did hope and hope and *hope* that no one would ask for it first!

At last, after what seemed hours, Jimmie's turn came to make his choice.

"Jimmie Mackay!" called out the lady by the tree.

Jimmie jumped from his seat like a shell from a cannon. All he could see was the red fire engine; it was still there!

As he approached the lady he noticed that she was the very one who had spoken to him in the street and given him his ticket for the party. Immediately a new idea entered his mind.

"And what would you like to have, Jimmie?" asked the lady. "You may have any one thing you like from the tree."

What an offer! Jimmie could scarcely take it in. He stood and gazed up at the sparkling, heavily laden tree. Once more his eye caught sight of the fire engine.

"Most of all," he said, looking up at the lady, "I would like that red fire engine; but if you don't mind, I will take that doll over there."

Tears filled his eyes as he said it, but with great resolution he kept his face straight.

Somehow the lady seemed to understand, and without a word she brought Jimmie the doll. As he went away, she squeezed his hand, and bending down, whispered, "God bless you, Jimmie."

But the other children did not understand at all. For a moment all restraint broke down, as with whoops and yells they told the world that Jimmie had chosen a doll. Some of the boys called out "Sissy!" and others, with a laugh, "Imagine a boy taking a doll!" And the little girls said, "That was just the doll we wanted!"

Jimmie blushed. He couldn't help it. Finally he became so uncomfortable that he put on his cap and went out, with the doll under his arm.

All the way home he thought about the bad luck that seemed to have dogged his footsteps that evening. First, he had lost his fire engine, and second, he had been laughed at by the whole crowd of children.

"If I'm not the unluckiest feller—" he began. Then he felt the doll under his arm. At once his thoughts brightened and his step quickened.

A few minutes later he was up in the little dark bedroom where Jean lay sick in bed.

"I'm so glad you have come!" said Jean. "It's so lonely here all by myself. And what have you got there?" she asked, sitting up in bed and peering at the doll with eager eyes. "Is that for me? Oh, Jimmie, Jimmie, you *are* a dear!"

Jimmie forgot all about his bad luck. A thrill of joy went through him as he saw his sister's delight.

Just then there was a knock at the door. It was the lady from the meeting. "What—" began Jimmie.

"I've come to say how sorry I am that the children were so unkind to you this evening," interrupted the lady. "They are sorry, too, now. I told them why you chose the doll. And they asked me to bring you something for yourself. Here it is. Now I must go, for it is getting late. Good night!" And she was gone.

Jimmie gasped, and then opened the package.

It was the fire engine!

Then he danced a jig around Jean's bed, chuckling to himself, and saying?

"If I ain't the luckiest feller that ever lived!"

Christmas Echo

LES THOMAS

Each of us wears a mask, a mask which is a false front to what we really are. Not even do those dearest and closest to us truly know all that we are deep within the labyrinths of our troubled souls.

And pain is universal in the human race; it seems to be an inexorable law of our planet that sooner or later great happiness is followed by great sorrow. It's almost like there is a universal score-

keeper somewhere tabulating, tabulating, tabulating—when the score gets too lopsided . . . CRASH! The roof caves in.

In this wondrous story, Thomas creates a misty rainbow through the veil of tears. It was only a moment, but some moments are worth several lifetimes.

"Good evening and happy holidays. The temperature is thirty-five degrees under cloudy skies. The National Weather Service forecasts a thirty percent chance of snow tonight. It could be the first white Christmas on record here in forty-one years."

The radio voice startled the old man who had been asleep in his stuffed chair by the fireplace. He coughed and rubbed his face and stared at the coals that rose and fell in halfhearted, tiny flames.

One word fixed his attention on the broadcast. Snow.

"That's always what they say," he muttered to himself. "But I don't see how it can happen. Not cold enough. I doubt it. I doubt it very much."

Still, the prospect was enough to make him stretch and get up unsteadily. He walked slowly over the bare living room floor and pulled back the drapes to look out over the lawn. Across the street, red, green, and yellow lights sparkled on the roof of the Williams's house and outlined the picture window in front of a flocked white tree. The old man could see Williams—his young daughter in his arms—and his wife finishing the last of the tree's decorations. A north wind brushed the trees and frosted up the window where he stood. The old man craned his neck to look as far as he could in both directions. There was not a trace of a snowflake.

He turned around and his gaze fell for a moment on the photograph in the silver frame on top of the piano. There were two people in the picture. One was a pleasant-looking woman with brown hair who was dressed in an old-fashioned heavy winter coat and high shoes. The other was a girl of about six. In the photograph, the woman and the child were holding hands. They were standing in snow.

Brubaker was seventy-two years old. A long time ago, he promised himself that he would try to not think so much about the people in the photograph. But each Christmas it was a promise he never tried to keep. He walked over and sat down again and stared at the remnants of the fire. Ordinarily Brubaker disliked daydreams. It was a lesson he had learned. Bad to let the mind wander. Bad to dream. He came to accept that in a way that had changed him slowly, almost imperceptibly, in grades of lessening rage in the years that passed after he lost Emily and Julie.

Eventually, Brubaker was able to accept death. *"Yes,"* he thought, *"death is reality. It is truth."* It was life that he could no longer trust. "Only a fool would believe in it," he ranted once, "and if you do, life will drive you crazy."

He came to believe those things not suddenly, but over the space of many years. With music, it was different. He gave that up almost immediately.

The day after the accident Brubaker resigned his job as band director of the high school. Later, he took a job at the mill, glad to be able to drown the melody that was his life in the cacophony of pounding hammers and forges. Out, too, without remorse, went the piles of records. One day he very calmly took a hammer and smashed to bits all of the black discs that he and Emily had so carefully scrimped to buy. Then he collected all the sheet music and the manuscripts and quickly shredded them, too. It all lay in a heap—the whole sweet serenade of the thirties, all of Harry James, the Dorseys, Glenn Miller, and Artie Shaw.

Two things survived the purge of music in Brubaker's life. One was Emily's piano. The other was a silver trumpet that rested in its cover on a shelf of the bedroom closet. Brubaker could not explain why he kept them. In fact, he had once tried to rid himself of them, too, but he found himself going after them later, with embarrassment, asking to buy them back. He told himself they were not really instruments capable of making music anymore, but only monuments. Silent monuments. And they were relics that no longer had souls or hearts. That part of them was finished. Never again, Brubaker decided, would they play melodies to taunt and remind him of the deception of happiness that had ended in such unbearable catastrophe.

Feeling chill, Brubaker shivered suddenly and coughed. He got up and walked into the kitchen, found the prescription bottle, and slowly drained the last drops into a teaspoon. He glanced at the kitchen clock. It was almost nine. *"Perhaps it is not too late,"* he thought, *"to get this refilled."* Brubaker got a telephone book from the drawer, took his glasses out of the pocket of his sweater, and absentmindedly put them on. He leafed through the pages: "Pawn shops . . . pet supplies . . . pharmacies. Hall's Drugs . . . Town Drugstore . . . Smith's Pharmacy."

Rheumatic and far past the age of normal retirement, Samuel Benjamin Smith stooped over greatly and his head bobbed when he walked. Beneath starch white hair, he wore old-fashioned bifocals that perched continually on the end of his nose and whenever anything happened out of the ordinary, Sam Smith's eyes would slowly elevate above the lenses like search beacons looking for whatever was the matter.

The beacons were on when Sam hung up the telephone. He turned around with his head bobbing and slowly began poking through the inventory along the back shelves of the druggist's room in the back of the ancient drugstore.

Out in front, Billy was sweeping away the last debris of the Christmas Eve rush when he heard Sam call him. Seventeen years old and a senior in high school, Billy was rounding out three years as an employee of Smith's Drugstore. He liked the job. Many times, Sam had told him he was the best helper he ever had. Even customers said Billy was a natural for the drugstore business.

He already even had an offer of a full scholarship in science at the state college. After that, there would be pharmacy school. Who knows, he might even take over the business from Sam. Billy thought so. After all, he had a natural talent for it.

The only thing he could do as well was play the horn. He was first chair in the school stage band. He even played trumpet with a group of older guys who played weekend dances. But you can't make a living with that kind of music. Those days were gone and Billy knew it. Still, it was fun to fool around. Mentally, he thought of a difficult piece the group had been working on as he hurried off to the back of the store.

Sam was filling a small brown bottle with a syrupy mixture. "Looks like you'll have to make one last delivery," Sam said, looking up. "I want you to take this over to Ed Brubaker on Oak Street. It's the old brick house on the corner across from the depot." Sam twisted the cap on the bottle and looked slowly over the top of his glasses to study Billy, who was whistling softly the practice tune that was running through his mind. He stopped whistling when he saw Sam look up.

"Now *there* was a musician," Sam said, shaking his head, tapping the bottle of cough syrup. "Old Ed Brubaker when he was a young man could play with the best of them. Why there was talk he even had an offer to go to New York with one of the big bands. They played real music in those days. Music was Ed's whole life. You never saw a happier fellow. He even got the high school band to sounding like a big orchestra. Those fellows were always giving the town a serenade. Ed saw to it there was always music. Easter, the Fourth of July . . . all the holidays, Ed always had the band right there. But the best of it, the very best, was always

Christmas Eve. That was special. They'd all pile in those old cars and go up to the mountain. Everybody in town used to wait up to hear it. Just before midnight, Ed would raise up that trumpet and then he'd start to play, real low at first, so low you thought you were dreaming it, and then it'd get louder. Lord, it was music so sweet you'd have bet it was Gabriel himself calling you.

"And then they'd fire off that old cannon from the school, right at the stroke of midnight. And that was how it happened. Let's see, it was Christmas 1933, no, 1934. Terrible thing. Maybe it was the cold and the snow that caused it. They never did know. That cannon just blew up in their faces. Ed was the only one who wasn't hurt. The explosion killed three people. One was a girl from the high school. The others were Ed's wife and his little daughter. It was a terrible thing to happen. Just terrible. Afterward, Ed barely said a word again to anybody, even after all these years. And he never played music again."

Outside, Billy shivered in the chilly wind and climbed on the delivery bicycle to ride the four blocks and make his delivery. On the way, he thought about the things Sam told him about the man who was waiting for the package in his pocket. He made the block through the business section in front of stores still crowded with late shoppers and cut down through residential streets in the old part of town. The icy wind stung his face and he pulled his woolen cap lower. It was freezing, but he was in no special hurry to meet this sad man on the eve of Christmas.

Finally, he turned onto Oak and pulled up in the driveway of the small brick house with a steep high roof. The trim of the house was green and the brick was dark red and it was set near the front of an immaculate yard and hedges, carefully manicured, Billy supposed, by someone with a lot of time on his hands.

The man who answered was wearing a heavy sweater and baggy wool trousers. When he reached through the door to take the package, Billy saw him fumble for a minute, then drop a metal object into his pocket, as if to hide it. Still, Billy recognized instantly that the old man had been holding a trumpet mouthpiece in his hand. The thought of it flashed in his mind like an incongruous piece of a puzzle. He was intrigued by the mystery of it. While the old man counted out the change, the delivery boy looked at him and tried to think of the words that might unlock part of the mystery. He wanted to say something. Anything. But what? Then it was too late. He watched the old man take a wrinkled five dollar bill from his pocket, fold it once, and put it in his hand. "This is for you," he said, "and Merry Christmas."

Billy took the long way back. He turned up through the business district, past the square. The stores were closing now and the streets were almost empty. He turned the corner and saw a young couple swinging a little girl between their arms. The child giggled with delight and the couple laughed. Billy rode past the square another block and turned east toward home.

In the kitchen, Brubaker unscrewed the cap and poured another teaspoon of the cough medicine. He put the bottle in the cupboard and glanced again at the clock. Then he turned around, walked slowly into the living room, and took his heavy coat from the closet. Unlatching the back door, he flipped on the porchlight that lighted the little courtyard garden in back, and walked out and sat down on the garden bench.

Brubaker leaned back and closed his eyes, letting his thoughts drift back to Christmases of long ago, Christmases that might have been. He tried to picture the three of them together, laughing, happy. Brubaker sighed heavily and shrugged. In his hands, the silver trumpet reflected in the moonlight. The wind had slowed now and the night was still and quiet. It was almost midnight. Brubaker closed his eyes again. Then he heard it.

It was very faint at first, so soft Brubaker thought he might be dreaming, but then he knew he wasn't. The notes were clear and mellow, ringing like wisps of wind, coming unmistakably from the mountain. With each bar of the Christmas carol, the trumpet's call seemed to grow, like a choir adding voices, like the triumphant march of a musical army. Brubaker felt his emotions welling with each note, till the tears finally flooded his cheeks. Then, like a man in a dream, he picked up the trumpet and, lifting it to his lips, began to play an echo to the mountain serenade, a salute to the unseen musician. Together, the two voices in harmony soared over the notes, calling each to the other's call and showering the silent city with a serenade.

After a long while at the top of the mountain, Billy could still hear the echo pounding in his ears when he reached down and closed the snaps of his trumpet case.

Across town, when the music ended, Sam Smith went over to a window and looked out across his lawn.

"Melinda, come see," he said. "It's snowing."

Running Away from Christmas

ANNIE HAMILTON DONNELL

Ever feel like running away from Christmas, somewhere where there is no evidence that it even exists? Well, that's the way Katharine Kane felt, so she abducted her long-suffering husband, Anthony, and they fled—with entirely unexpected and far-reaching results. . . . Over a hundred years ago, it was—but it might just as well have been today.

Annie Hamilton Donnell was a

frequent contributor to most of the family magazines of America and England during the early years of the twentieth century. She almost had been forgotten. She is well worth rediscovering.

"Sit down, Anthony, right here on the hall bench, before you take off your coat. Dinner isn't ready, anyway, and I've time to tell you something. It's—it's my ultimatum. I think that's what you call it."

The face of Anthony Kane, softened and stirred by his wife's kiss, stiffened into astonishment. What was this Kitty had to say, solemn enough to merit "Anthony" and "ultimatum"? Kitty rarely greeted him with big words.

"You needn't be scared, dear, though *I* am! I frighten myself—but I shall do it. I have spent all day deciding: And you know, when I *decide*, Anthony—"

"Oh, come, call me by my right name!"

"Well, Tony, then. Sit down. You look so big standing up, and I feel specially little with this on my mind. Tony, we'll run away from Christmas."

"We'll—what?"

"Run away. It will be simple enough; only we must

run in time. I've got our things nearly packed. You needn't say a syllable." Her cool fingers were over his lips. "I'm doing the saying. I have it all planned right down to the single detail of where to run to. It's got to be someplace where there isn't a thought of Christmas; that's all I stipulate. We'll keep on running till we get to That Place."

"Katharine!"

"Call me Kitty. Yes, dear?"

"You never told me there was insanity in your family. This isn't giving a fellow a square deal."

"Well, there is insanity," returned his small, cool wife. "It comes on periodically. We are all taken crazy just about this time o' year, and we gradually recover after Christmas. This year I am going to skip my attack. And you've got to 'skip' with me." She laughed enjoyingly at her modest pun. Her hand crossed and recrossed Anthony Kane's shaven cheek, with the lingering and tender touch of childless wives who have so much time to caress husbands' cheeks.

"Think of not having to do up the bundles, Tony, not one bundle! No flurry and scurry and scolding each other at the last minute; no tissue paper and ribbon and strings and writing addresses. Just you and me"—Kitty was not always hampered by grammatic rule—"sitting comfortably together in That Place, wherever it is, the No-Christmas Place we are going to run away to."

He attempted to restore her sanity by homely suggestion. "Let's run away to dinner," he soothed. "If I'm not mistaken, I smell a Belinda potpie—"

"We'll start anyway day after tomorrow. I suppose you will have to have time to wind up your affairs. Tony, if I never had an inspiration before, this is one. And to think of all the dreading and planning I might have saved! I spent *hours* trying to reckon how we stand with the Smith-Curtises, and what we'd got to spend on the Dana Wards this year."

She sprang lightly to her feet and faced him.

"Christmas!" she scorned, all her sweet face aflame. "Merry Christmas! Anthony Kane, we've been married eleven years, eleven weary Christmases full of nervous prostration and empty pocketbooks and—tissue paper, and *strings!* Trying to keep up our end of things and give folks as valuable presents as they gave us last year! I don't know what you call it; I call it a give-and-take scramble, and I've had enough of it. There's no way out of it but to run away. I don't want to see or hear a word of Christmas, and there must be a place somewhere. We'll take hold of hands, dear, and find it. Now we'll have dinner."

But she drifted back to him as he hung up his coat. The tone that penetrated into that little closet was a tone he knew, but rarely had heard. He did not need to look at Kitty's broken little face.

"Of course—of course I'd have *loved* Christmas if we'd ever hung up little stockings; do you think I'd run away from that?" And she was gone again. There had never been little stockings.

Two days later they were actually on their way to That Place beyond the reach of Christmas. It was characteristic of Katharine Kane that the wild little plan had materialized; she was accustomed to carry through her plans. To Anthony Kane, her husband, to whom she was wife and children and all the world, submission even to crazy little schemes came easily. He had fortunately leisure and wherewithal to indulge her.

"Well, we've started for somewhere, Puss, but how do you know you won't find a Christmas there? We may run right into it."

"Don't laugh; this is sober earnest. Honestly, Tony, I am so sick of the present-day mercenary, distorted kind of celebrating that I want to *rest;* yes, I do! I want to forget it. You're a dear, not to mind anything, not even being pulled up by the roots at a moment's notice. When I get home, I shall give *you* a Christmas present." The inconsistency of woman! "But just now we are on the way to a place called Hardscrabble. I picked it out on a timetable. You don't look for a Christmas there, do you?" She laughed, not without modest pride at her "find." "But if anything happens that we 'run into' one, as you predict, I've two other promising places on my list: Starkville and World's End—what do you say to going to those? The last one isn't on a railroad; we'll have to hire a sleigh, and hunt it up. I happened to see a reference to it in the newspaper. Oh Tony, aren't you beginning to have a lovely time? Just us two!"

"Great! Real Christmas spirit," mumbled Tony. He was in reality not averse to this remarkable escapade. He and Kitty deserved a little freedom after their eleven proper and expensive Christmases.

He did not really accept her pessimistic theory of the utter demoralization of Christmas; in Anthony Kane's still youthful mind were too many blissful memories, but he "accepted" Kitty. Poor child, she had been a little solitary up to the time he had found her; and from that time on had occurred the wearisome annual games of give and take that had occasioned this adventurous quest. Kitty had much to excuse her. He never forgot the denied sweets of motherhood that she had missed.

"But look here." It was considerably farther on in the trip; an uncomfortable thought had just occurred to him. "Kitty, how will it look?"

" 'Look'? Oh Tony, you waked me up, and I was starting in on such a beautiful dream! How will what 'look,' dear?"

"This—this freak of ours. Everybody'll send us the costly rubbish just the same. I don't like the taste of the thought, Katharine."

"I've fixed that part, of course. We shall not find the front porch piled with bundles, man, dear; go on with your newspaper. I dropped a hint with Celia Beede, and I waited till she picked it up, too. Celia is so dependable!"

Hardscrabble proved a sightly little town set on a hill. It had a suspicious look of a certain amount of thrift and cheer, even in the gloom of its ill-lighted little streets. They were driven in silence to its one hotel, Katharine's spirits oddly damped. Well, all there was about it—there were the two other places! She would put into immediate action her investigations. If Hardscrabble proved a disappointment— it was destined to do it.

After the ambitious little meal called "supper," Katharine disappeared. It was half an hour later when she broke in upon Anthony sitting in the hot little bedroom.

"Oh, you've got your coat off! Put it on quick; our train goes in fifteen minutes! There's a sleeper on it. You shall have a good night's rest, poor boy. I'm doing the best I can for you."

"But what—"

"We can't stay here, Tony. This place is *full* of Christmas! I've been out investigating. The shop windows are all

61

lighted up and decorated—actually decorated! And about every house has Christmas wreaths in the windows. Hurry, dear! I'll shut up the bags."

At Starkville, when by devious ways they finally arrived at that dreary-sounding place, they were met upon the little station platform with no less than three "Merry Christmases." More of them, cheery and friendly, greeted them at the Starkville House. It appeared to be a Christmassy little spot.

"Now, isn't it too bad? You'll have to put up with a top-floor room, and a back one at that! But we're full, because of Christmas. The band folks always put up with us, and we always have a band here for the rally."

" 'Rally'?" But Katharine did not look at Anthony. Already she tasted new defeat. In a species of despair she clutched Anthony's arm and walked out.

"Never mind, Puss; better luck next time," comforted that soothing person. "There's your third place— End o' the World, is it? We haven't given that a trial. If we run into Christmas there, we'll change our tactics and call it our wedding trip. We never really had one, and it's nobody's business when or where we go."

"Oh, you're a dear!" she sighed. "No other woman's husband would have come off like this, anyway, just to please a frantic wife."

Kitty was travelworn and in her secret soul a little repentant of her lunacy. Even a Christmas-harried, bundle-littered home looked appealing to her tonight. But because she was Kitty it did not occur to her to turn back from her undertaking. She had undertaken to find a Christmasless place and spend her Christmas in it. Besides, she hadn't run away from Tony.

"Let's have supper," she cried briskly. "Let's be happy, dear! Just us two at a little table here at the end of the world. Then we'll go to the real World's End. We're *due* there, Tony—you don't mind?"

"Me, mind?" Tony was just getting into the spirit of things. He had the windy little sense of having eloped with Kitty; and the farther they ran, the better. Had he ever really had her to himself before?

After supper they continued their adventurous journeying to World's End.

"I think," Kitty mused aloud, "that we've been harnessed up, with the overdraw checkrein and all that, you know, and driven in little narrow roads that other people made for us, and we didn't dare to turn out of. We're—we're unchecked now, and—out to grass!" She laughed enjoyingly. "Doesn't it seem good to get our heads down, and *browse?*" He stooped suddenly and kissed her.

World's End had been properly named; but they succeeded in finding it, and the night before Christmas found them in the primitive little settlement of a half dozen houses and a blacksmith shop. That round a bend in the road a little farther on they would have found more houses and a general store they refused to be told; this was the World's End they wanted. It satisfied Kitty; she saw no signs of Christmas. The elderly soul in one of the houses who agreed to take them in did not wish them a merry Christmas. The elderly man soul who appeared to belong to her wore a serious, un-Christmas countenance. There were no holly wreaths visible anywhere, and the blacksmith shop was undecorated.

"We've found the Place," Kitty whispered, but she boasted too soon. Two hours later she realized her mistake.

Tony had gone to bed in the company room of the little house; but Kitty, with a woman's uneasiness and her own particular gift of wakefulness, had remained up with a book from one of the suitcases.

"Tony! Tony!" Her lips were close to his ear, and she was gently shaking him. She had just returned from a little excursion to the kitchen for a drink.

"Tony, they've hung their stockings up—their poor old stockings!" Kitty was crying, though she did not know it, and could scarcely have told why, if she had known. "Get up, dear! Tony, please! Help me find something nice of yours for the solemn old-man stocking. I know of something for the other one."

So it came about that a few minutes later these two, who had run away from Christmas, stole, stocking-footed, out to the small, drear kitchen to play Santa Claus.

"Let a little end hang over the top, so he'll see it first thing. It's your prettiest tie; Tony, you're a dear; Tony, if you dare to laugh at me!" But he was not laughing.

As they sat at breakfast the next morning, a little trail of humble vehicles paraded past the window; and the old person waiting upon them explained it. She was suddenly excited.

"Ezry! Ezry! It's goin' past! Don't stop to wipe your face!" she called to her old husband in a room beyond. "It's Mis' Blacksmith Avery, her that was young Ellen Till," she explained to her guests. "Isn't it a pity to be buried on Christmas Day? And Blacksmith Avery *Thanksgiving!* I tell *him* it should have been us; we wouldn't have left two little mites."

"Oh, two little mites!" breathed Kitty. Her fork slipped with a soft clatter to her plate. She sat forward in her chair, her eyes on the tail of the somber little procession going by.

"Two, yes; I suppose it's a mercy there weren't six; but I declare it's hard to see some mercies. They're little

65

dears; Ellen was a beautiful girl. There isn't any better stock anywhere round here than Till stock, and I don't know but Avery comes next. I have never seen politer little dears."

"Oh, little dears!" Kitty murmured. Tony did not venture to look at the troubled little face of her. He felt the stirrings of her denied and hungry soul.

The old voice ran on garrulously. It was rare it found so good a chance as this.

"Fond o' children, are you?" The old eyes had come to rest on Kitty's face. "Well, then, I guess you'd be fond o' these children! If you'd like to see them, I'll go over with you. The poor farm's coming after them this afternoon. We better go soon."

But Kitty had already gone, alone. The old woman's gaze followed her admiringly.

"Isn't she spry? Well, I tell him to look at the way I used to go around instead o' looking at me now. Yes, we've got to let the poor farm take the Blacksmith Avery children." She sighed. "There is no one else to take them, and there isn't a grain o' money to keep them if there was. 'Twon't be much different for them, poor dears, than for the rest of us. All of us live on poor farms."

Anthony Kane was not surprised that Kitty did not

66

come back alone. He went a little way along the snowy road to meet her, and now he looked at Kitty's face. It was lighted softly by some inner light, the light he knew.

"This is 'Son,' and this is 'Sister,' " she introduced quietly. "They are both so little, Tony!"

"Sister is; I ain't. I'm big," the little voice of Son piped eagerly. "When I'm 'leven months older, I'll be seven. I–I mean I was *goin'* to be if mother hadn't died."

"I want mother!" suddenly broke in baby wailing from the tremulous lips of the other child. Sister in 'leven months more could not be more than four. Her round, wholesome little face was grotesquely contorted with its grief. To Anthony Kane, looking down, it was a piteous little face.

"Man, dear—"

"Yes, Puss. Yes, I know."

"Both, Anthony? How can a little Son live without a little Sister?"

But he was spared decision. Son was before him.

"She's goin' to take me, an' I'm goin' to take Sister, an' we're goin' to have a Chris'mas. You tell him," pushing Kitty forward. "Tell him he can kiss Sister; the best place is under her chin."

To Tony, Son gravely explained: "I promised to let her

67

kiss me 'leven more months, but she better do it on my hair; that's the cleanest place. Can I pray Sister nights? I promised mother I would."

Katharine Kane on her knees gathered the two of them into her arms. It was as if they were "praying" her. A long time afterward, it seemed, she heard Anthony's voice, striving for matter-of-factness.

"There's a train on that little branch at one o'clock. If we could catch it—"

"Of course we can catch it! If we have to run all the four miles! We've got to hurry home, Tony, on account of Christmas. We'll be a day or two late, but we'll catch it!"

She dropped her voice to an eager whisper. "Little stockings," she breathed. "We've got to hurry home and hang them up."

And again they were off, but this time, they were running after Christmas.

The Promise of the Doll

RUTH C. IKERMAN

Few stories I have shared equal the impact of this short little story. Born in that now vanished magazine, Christian Herald, *and reprinted in* Guideposts Magazine, *it has gradually become a part of many families' Christmas season.*

It reminds us that the act of giving does something to us: ennobles and changes us—in proportion to the sacrifice parting with the gift represents.

When I met my friend on the crowded street, she held out her hand to me and said, "I hope you can help me. I'm desperate." Wearily she explained, "I'm about to cry and it's all over a doll. I simply have to find this doll for my granddaughter."

As tears filled her eyes, I remembered the terrible shock we all had felt over the death of her daughter, who had been such a vivacious young mother until stricken several months before. The young husband was doing a fine job with the little girl, but it was on the grandmother that much of the burden of planning for good things remained. And this explained her Christmas errand.

"I blame myself entirely," she told me, "for not starting earlier but I never thought it would be a problem to find one of these special dolls. Yet there is not one of this variety left in town."

I asked her, "Well, why can't you settle for another kind of doll?"

She shook her head. "One of the last things my daughter ever said to me before the pain got so bad was how sorry she was that she had refused to buy this doll for her little girl. She told me she had thought the child was too young for such a doll, and had refused to buy it for her birthday, supposing there were lots of occasions ahead when she could get it for her."

Then she told the rest of the story. The little girl had come to her mother's bedside and asked whether the doll might arrive at Christmastime. The young mother grasped the tiny hand in hers and said, "I promise you this for Christmas." Then she had asked her own mother to do this one thing, "Just make sure that my little girl gets that doll this Christmas."

Now my friend was about to fail in her mission. "It's all my fault," she kept repeating. "I waited until too late. It will take a miracle now."

Secretly I agreed, but I tried to keep up a polite facade of courage. "Maybe the child has forgotten, and will be happy with something else."

Grimly my friend replied, "*She* may forget, but I won't." We parted to go our separate ways.

With my mind only half on my shopping, I found the ribbon a neighbor wanted to finish a baby blanket she was making. A few minutes later I stopped at her door to leave the package and was invited inside.

Her two little girls sat on the floor, playing with their

dolls. As I sat down, I noticed that one of the dolls was the same type my friend was seeking. Hopefully I asked, "Can you remember where you bought that doll?"

My neighbor gave me her warmhearted smile. "That's not a doll," she said, "she's a member of the family, and as near as I can see she probably was born and not made. She came to us by plane from a favorite aunt in the East."

So I told her that I had a friend who was searching frantically for such a doll for the little girl whose mother had passed away during the year. Apparently unaware of us, the two children played happily. The mother and I spoke in adult words about facing loss at the holiday time, and how much we wished we could help my friend.

Later when I got up to leave, the two little girls followed me to the door.

"Dolly is ready to leave, too," they told me. Sure enough, she was dressed in a red velveteen coat and hat with a white fur muff.

"Where is dolly going?" I asked.

They laughed happily. "With you, of course. You know where the lady lives, don't you—the one who needs the doll so bad?"

I started to tell them that of course I couldn't take this doll. Then I looked at their faces, happy in the moment of giving. If I say the wrong thing now, something within

74

my heart warned, I may ruin their joy of giving for the rest of their lives. Silently I took the doll, fumbling with my car keys so they did not see the mist over my eyes.

Their mother asked, "Are you both sure you want to do this?" They answered, "Yes, we do." The mother put her arms around them tenderly.

Later I rang the doorbell of my friend. "Don't ask me how I got it, for I can't talk just yet. The doll is a little smudgy, but the worn places are from kisses and maybe they won't show under the Christmas lights."

She fondled the doll as though it were made of precious metal. Tears of joy welled up in the woman's eyes when I finally was able to tell the story.

"How can I ever thank those children enough?" she asked.

"They already have received a blessing greater than anything you or I could give them," I told her. "I saw their faces when they offered me the doll to bring to you."

And it was true. In the moment of giving they had also received, in ways past our finding out. A miracle had taken place. A promise could be kept, linking here with there, in the eternal circle of love of which the great gift of Christmas itself is a part.

The Fir Tree Cousins

�֍

LUCRETIA D. CLAPP

If gifts are merely perfunctory, of what value are they? To pretty Ann Brewster, who gave such gifts, not much; and to those who received them, even less.

But this Christmas. . . .

This old story dates clear back to the early years of this century, a time when presents were nailed in wooden boxes rather than taped in cardboard boxes as we do today.

Pretty Mrs. Brewster sat in the middle of her bedroom floor, surrounded by a billowy mass of tissue paper, layers of cotton batting, bits of ribbon, tinsel, and tags. She was tying up packages of various shapes and sizes, placing each one when finished in a heaped-up pile at one side. Her face was flushed; wisps of cotton clung to her dress and hair, and she glanced up anxiously now and then at the little clock on the desk as it ticked off the minutes of the short December afternoon.

"I'll never be through—*never!*" she remarked disconsolately after one of these hurried glances. "And there's the box for cousin Henry's family that just *must* go tonight, and the home box. Oh, Nancy Wells—" She broke off suddenly as she caught sight of a slender little figure standing in the doorway, surveying her with merry brown eyes.

"Nancy Wells! Come right in here. You're as welcome as—as the day after Christmas!"

"So you've reached that stage, have you, Ann?" the visitor laughed as she picked her way carefully across the littered floor to an inviting wicker chair near the fire.

"Yes, I have. You know I always begin to feel that way

just about this time, Nancy, only it seems to be a mite worse than usual this year."

Ann Brewster stretched out one cramped foot and groaned. "Here I am just slaving, while you—well, you look the very personification of elegant leisure. I suspect every single one of those forty-nine presents on your regular list is wrapped, and tied and labeled and mailed, too, if mailed it has to be. Well, you can just take off your coat and hat, Nancy, fold yourself up Turk-like on the floor here, and help me out. I've an appointment at four-thirty, and it's nearly that now. I'm not nearly through, but I just must finish today. If there's one thing I'm particular about, Nancy, it is that a gift shall reach the recipient on time. For my part, I don't want a Christmas present a week cold, so to speak, nor even a day. And somehow, I always manage to get mine off, even if I do half kill myself doing it."

" 'Do your Christmas shopping early,' " quoted Nancy, mischievously, as she seated herself obediently on the floor.

"Yes; and 'only five more shopping days,' "Ann smiled ruefully. "Why don't you go on? Those well-meant little reminders I've had flaunted in my face everytime I've stepped into a store or picked up a daily paper for the past six weeks. They have come to be as familiar as the street sign out there on that lamp-post—and receive about the same amount of attention, too."

"Well, after all, Ann, it is a delightful sort of rush, now isn't it? I'm willing to admit that I'd miss it all dreadfully."

Nancy Wells looked about her appreciatively at the chintz-hung room glowing in the warmth of the open wood fire, and with its pleasant disarray of snowy paper and gay ribbons.

"My, but that's a lovely package!" she remarked, as Ann cut a square of tissue paper and measured a length of silver cord. "And what a clever idea that is! I should never have thought of using cotton batting and a sprinkling of diamond dust for the top layer."

"Well, you see, Nancy, this is for Cousin Harriet. She has everything anyone could possibly wish for, and she always sends me such beautiful things that I make a special effort to have my gift to her as dainty as possible and a little different."

Ann paused and glanced at the clock.

"My, look what time it is! I'll have to go. I wonder if you'd just as soon stay, Nancy, and finish up that little pile over there by the couch. They're for the fir tree cousins down on the farm."

"The *fir* tree cousins! Whatever do you mean, Ann?"

Ann laughed gaily as she stood up and shook off the bits of tinsel and ribbon from her skirt.

"Oh, I always call them that in fun," she explained. "They're Tom's cousins that live down in Maine. The idea struck me, I suppose, because theirs is the 'Country of the Pointed Firs,' you know. I've never seen any of them, but I've always sent them a box at Christmas ever since I've been married."

"What fun!" Nancy exclaimed enthusiastically. "How many are there, and what do you send them?"

"I don't know that I should call it *fun* exactly," Ann answered dubiously. "This buying gifts for people you've never seen and only know by hearsay is—well—not unalloyed. Let's see—there are Cousin Henry and Cousin Lucy, then the boys, Alec and Joe and little Henry, and one girl, Louise, who is just between the two older boys. And, oh, yes, there's Grandma Lewis, Cousin Lucy's mother."

Ann ticked off the names on her fingers.

"Yes, there are just seven of them. Tom says they have a fine farm. He used to go there summers when he was a boy. He just adores Cousin Lucy, and actually wanted to take me down there on our wedding trip. You can't accuse me of procrastination as far as they are concerned, Nancy, for I always buy their things long before any of the others. You see, I usually know just about what I'm going to send each one. I hit upon a certain thing and stick to it as nearly as possible every year. It's easier."

"Why, Ann, you don't give them the very same thing year after year, I hope?" Nancy looked up in comical dismay.

"Well, why not?" Ann demanded a trifle sharply. "Take Cousin Henry, for instance. I usually get a nice warm muffler for him, because I'm sure he can——"

"But I should think——" Nancy interrupted.

"My dear, it's just *freezing* cold there! They have terrible winters, and one needs mufflers—and more mufflers! You can't have too many. Then I nearly always pick out an apron of some kind for Cousin Lucy. One can't have too many aprons, either, especially when she does all her own work. For Grandma Lewis, I choose a bag or something to put her knitting in. This year I found some sort of an affair for holding the yarn. I didn't understand it very well myself, although they told me it was perfectly simple; but I thought an experienced knitter like Grandma Lewis would know how to use it. Louise is just sixteen, so it's easy enough to select a pair of stockings or a handkerchief for her. As for the boys, Alec and Joe, I always get them neckties—they can't have too many, you know—and for little Henry a game or toy of some kind. Then Tom adds a box of candy. Promptly one week after Christmas I receive a perfectly proper, polite letter from Cousin Lucy, thanking me in behalf of every

member of the fir tree household. It does sound a bit perfunctory, doesn't it, Nancy? Sort of a cut-and-dried perfor-
mance all around. Somehow, Christmas is getting to be
more and more like that every year; don't you think so? I
must confess I'm glad, positively relieved, when it's over!
I'm always a wreck, mentally as well as physically."

Nancy made no comment; instead she pointed with
the scissors to a heap of large and small packages over at
one side.

"What do you want done with those, Ann?"

"Oh, they go in the home box. That has to go tonight,
too. I was just starting to tie them up. Do you suppose
you'd have time to do them too, Nancy dear? I know I'm
just imposing on you. Just put the two piles on my bed
when you've finished wrapping, will you? Then Tom can
pack them after dinner. Now I'm off. Good-bye, and thanks
awfully."

A minute later Nancy Wells heard the front door
slam, then the house settled down to an empty quiet, broken only by the rustling of tissue paper and the click of scissors as Nancy folded and cut and measured and snipped.
The fire burned to a bed of dull embers; and beyond the
small square windowpanes, the snow-lit landscape dark-
ened to dusk.

"There!" said Nancy, as she gave a final pat to the last

bow. "And how pretty they look, too," she added, leaning back to survey her handiwork. Then she carried them over to the bed and arranged them in two neat piles.

"Certainly looks like 'Merry Christmas,' all right." With which remark, she put on her coat and hat and went home.

It was several hours later that Ann Brewster surveyed with weariness, compounded with relief, the empty spaces on bed and floor. The last label had been pasted on while Tom stood by with hammer and nails, ready to perform the final offices. And the two boxes, the one for the fir tree cousins down on the Maine farm, the other for Ann's own family in Michigan, were now on their way to the down-town office.

"And now that's over for another year at least," she sighed. "And I'm too tired to care much whether those boxes reach their destination safely or not. Twelve months from tonight, in all probability, I shall be sitting in this same spot making that very same remark. And I used to just *love* Christmas, too."

Ann Brewster (she was Ann Martin then) had been brought up in a family where there had been little money to spare, even for necessities. Nevertheless, Mr. and Mrs. Martin had always contrived to make the day and the season itself one of happy memory to their four children. No elaborate celebration of later years ever held quite the same degree of delight and anticipation shared then by every member of the family. Ann recalled the weeks brimful of plans and mysterious secrets that preceded the day itself, with its simple gifts and its spirit of peace and good will toward all. Now it was so different!

"Tired, Ann?"

A masculine voice broke in on her reverie, and Tom's broad-shouldered figure filled the doorway.

"Cheer up! The boxes are on their way, or should be shortly, and a few days more will see the season's finish."

"That's just it, Tom. We're losing the spirit of Christmas—the simplicity and good wishes, I mean—that used to be the big thing about it."

Tom whistled thoughtfully, and when he spoke his voice had lost its merry banter. "I guess you're right there, Ann. We're certainly a long way off from the old days of five-cent horns and candy canes. A lot of that was youth, of course, but just the same this modern deal is all wrong. It's a selfish proposition, as I look at it. I don't believe I've ever told you, Ann, about a certain Christmas of mine, long ago. About the nicest I've ever known."

"Where was it? Do you mean at home?"

Ann looked up, interested.

"No." Tom's voice changed and a shadow crossed his

85

face. "You know I never had much of a home, Ann. My parents both died when I was only a little chap, and I was sort of parceled out to various relatives for different seasons of the year. No, this Christmas I'm thinking of was with Cousin Henry and Cousin Lucy. Queer I haven't told you before."

"I knew you spent your summers there," Ann answered a little curiously, "but I've never heard of your being there for Christmas."

"Well, I was, and I've never forgotten it. It was my first glimpse of what a real homey Christmas can be. The tree was just a homemade affair—that is, the trimmings. We cut the tree ourselves, a beautiful slender fir, and hauled it down on a sled from the hill back of the house. We popped corn and made wreaths, strung cranberries, and cut stars out of colored paper. And I tell you that tree was pretty—it wasn't glittering with ornaments and blazing with candles or electric lights."

"Did you have presents?" asked Ann.

"Yes, I remember Cousin Henry gave me a pair of homemade snowshoes. Grandma Lewis had knit some red wristlets for me, and Cousin Lucy a cap to match. I was the happiest boy in the State of Maine!"

Tom paused a moment. "But somehow, Ann, what I remember most was the spirit of the day itself. Cousin

Lucy had worked hard, I know, and in the evening had a lot of the neighbors in; but she was the life of the crowd. Ann, I'd like you to meet and really know Cousin Lucy. I wish she'd ask us to visit them sometime."

"Somehow, I never supposed—" Ann began hesitatingly.

"Supposed what?" Tom asked.

"Well, I guess I never gave your fir tree cousins much thought, Tom. I didn't think you cared particularly. You've never talked much about them nor made any effort to—"

"Yes, I know," Tom broke in, "and more's the shame to me, too. It's queer sometimes, that, no matter how much you may think of people, you just sort of drift apart. But you'd better get to bed now, Ann. You look tired to death."

The Thomas Brewsters faced each other across the breakfast table the morning after New Year's. There was a pile of letters beside Ann's plate.

"I know exactly what's in every one of these missives," she sighed.

Tom smiled as he opened his morning paper.

There was a silence for several minutes while Ann slowly slit the seals one by one. She picked up a square white envelope that bore her father's well-known handwriting, and a minute later a sudden exclamation made Tom look up.

"Why, Tom—Tom Brewster!"

Ann's eyes glanced down the single page; then she began to read aloud:

My dear Ann:

> *Perhaps you won't remember it, but you gave me a muffler for Christmas once long ago, when you were a very little girl. You picked it out yourself, and I'll say this—that you showed remarkable good taste. That muffler, or what's left of it, is tucked away somewhere in the attic now. The one you sent this year gives me almost as much pleasure as did that other one, although I suppose I'll have to concede that these new styles are really prettier (but not any warmer or more useful) than the old. Your mother thinks they must be coming back into favor again, but I don't care whether they are or not. They're warm and they help keep a clean collar clean. For my part, I'm glad we're getting*

away from the showy Christmases of the last few years
and down to a simpler, saner giving and receiving.
Lots of love and thanks to you and Tom.
Father.

Ann drew forth a small folded sheet that had been tucked inside the other one. It read:

Dear Ann,

I'm just going to add a line to put in with your father's, for we have a houseful of company and there's no time now for a real letter. Your box this year, although something of a surprise, was nonetheless welcome. I have thought for several years that we ought all of us to give simpler gifts. A remembrance, no matter how small, if carefully and thoughtfully chosen to meet the need or desire of the recipient, carries with it more of the real Christmas spirit than the costliest gift or one chosen at random. I don't know when I've had an apron given me before! I began to think they had gone out of fashion. I put yours right on, and your father said it made him think of when you children were little. The boys will write you themselves, but I'll

just say that Ned and Harold both remarked that they
were glad you sent them neckties. (You know we've
always tried to think up something different, with the
result that both are rather low on that article.) We've
had lots of fun with Hugh's game. He confided to me
that he'd been hoping somebody would give him one.
So you see, Ann, dear, we are all pleased with our
things and send you our grateful thanks. Love to you
both from

Mother.

P.S. I was afraid my letter telling of your Aunt
Cordelia's arrival had not reached you in time, but I
need not have worried. She was much taken with that
case for holding her yarn. She'd had one and lost it.
And Katy was real pleased with that pretty
handkerchief.

With a hand that trembled a little, and with burning
cheeks, Ann drew forth the last letter in the pile. It was
postmarked Maine, and contained two plain lined sheets,
tablet-size.

"This is from Cousin Lucy," Ann began, a queer little
note creeping into her voice:

My dear Ann:

When we opened your box on Christmas morning, I thought I had never seen anything so attractive. Seals and ribbons and greetings may not mean so much, perhaps, to you city people; but for us isolated ones, they add a great deal to our enjoyment and appreciation. Your gifts fulfilled certain long-felt desires, one or two of which I suspect are older than you are, Ann. Perhaps you cannot understand the joy of receiving something you've always wanted, yet did not really need. I am writing with my beautiful pin before me on the table. You see, it is the first one—the first really nice pin—I've ever owned. That is fulfilled desire number one. The second is the sight of your Cousin Henry enjoying a bit of leisure before the fire with his new book. I suppose Tom may have told you that once, as a young man, your Cousin Henry made this very trip to the headwaters of the Peace River. So few new and worthwhile books find their way to us. Louise and the boys will write later, so I'll only say that Alec actually takes his big flashlight to bed with him; Joe is inordinately proud of that safety razor; and as for little Henry—well, his father and I both feel that we ought to thank you on our own behalf, for all our efforts to make an out-of-door lad of him seem to have failed hitherto. He is the student of the family, but the new skates lure him outside and help to strike the proper balance. Louise loves her beaded bag, as, indeed, what girl wouldn't? And as for Grandma Lewis, she fairly flaunts that bit of rose point. She confided to me that at eighty years she had at last given up all hope of ever possessing a piece of real lace!

I have written a long letter, but I doubt if, after all, I've really succeeded in expressing even a small part of our appreciation to you and Tom for your carefully chosen gifts. To feel that a certain thing has been chosen especially for you, to fit your own individuality and particular desire, if not always need—this, it has always seemed to me, is the true spirit of Christmas. And I think you have found it, Ann. Before closing I want to ask if you and Tom can't arrange to make us a visit this summer?

Wishing you both a Happy New Year,

Lovingly,

Cousin Lucy.

Ann Brewster laid down the letter with something that was half a sob and half a laugh. "I'm just too ashamed to live!"

"Why, what's the matter, Ann?" Tom looked puzzled.

"Cousin Lucy speaks of my 'carefully chosen gifts.' And they weren't at all. They weren't even meant for any of them. You see"—Ann swallowed the lump in her throat—"I've always just chosen their things at random. Yes, I have, Tom. One of those Christmas obligations you spoke of the other night, to be disposed of with as little time and effort as possible. And then last week, when I was hurrying to get everything off, Nancy Wells came over and I left a lot of things for her to finish wrapping while I dashed off to the dressmaker's. And I suppose, in some way, I got the fir tree cousins' and the home pile mixed."

Tom pushed back his chair from the table.

"Seems to me, Ann dear, that we've had the answer to our query, 'What's wrong with Christmas?' You've sort of stumbled upon the truth this year, but—"

Tom stopped, whistling thoughtfully as he drew on his overcoat. There was a misty light in Ann's eyes as she stood beside him.

"When will you have your vacation, Tom?"

"August, probably."

"Well, we're going to spend it with our fir tree cousins! And, Tom, I can hardly wait!"

The Locking
In of Lisabeth

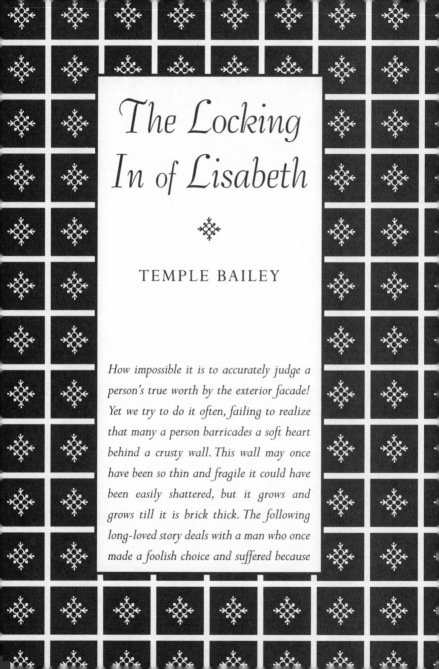

TEMPLE BAILEY

*How impossible it is to accurately judge a
person's true worth by the exterior facade!
Yet we try to do it often, failing to realize
that many a person barricades a soft heart
behind a crusty wall. This wall may once
have been so thin and fragile it could have
been easily shattered, but it grows and
grows till it is brick thick. The following
long-loved story deals with a man who once
made a foolish choice and suffered because*

of it for most of his adult lifetime. However, a chance encounter paved his way through the self-imposed wall and into the light.

Temple Bailey [?–1953], was one of America's most popular (and highest paid) writers early in this century. Both her stories and books had a huge readership. Little is known of her private life as she refused most interviews. She was a Presbyterian, and her writing reflects both this Christian perspective and her innate idealism.

Christmas was the same as any other day to Judge Blair. He lived alone and ate his Christmas dinner alone, and never gave presents. In fact, he was like the miller of Dee: For, since he cared for nobody, of course nobody cared for him.

On Christmas Eve the judge stayed late at his office. His clerks left at five.

"A Merry Christmas, Judge!" said Miss Jenkins, his stenographer, as she prepared to leave.

The judge looked up from his papers and stared at her over his glasses. "What's that? Oh, thank you, Miss Jenkins." But he did not return the greeting, and timid little Miss Jenkins blushed, and wondered if she had been too bold.

At half past six a waiter from a nearby restaurant brought in a light supper. The judge often supped at his office when he had an important case on hand. It saved time.

"A Merry Christmas, suh!" said the waiter, when he had arranged the tray in front of the old gentleman.

"Hum? Oh, ah, yeah—you may call for the tray later, George," said the judge, and George departed crestfallen; and if he banged the door on which was painted in imposing gilt letters MARCELLUS BLAIR, ATTORNEY-AT-LAW a little more vigorously than was necessary, why, who shall blame him?

The judge read over his brief while he ate, pausing now and then to pick up his lead pencil and make corrections in his neat legal hand. Suddenly he straightened up and looked around the room. "Now, what was that?" he murmured, looking over his eyeglasses.

Tap, tap, came a sound against the pane. He listened a moment and then went back to his work; but hearing it again, he rose and went to the window and raised the shade.

There was a narrow space between the building in which the judge had his offices on the fourth floor and the big public school next to it. But the snow sifted in between, and it was very dark.

Suddenly out of the blackness came the end of a long

wand, which hit the windowpane once, twice, quite sharply before the judge raised the sash with a bang. "Who's that?" he cried harshly.

"Please," said a very small voice across the way.

"Who's there?" asked the judge, peering into the darkness.

"It's me," said the little voice.

"Who's me?" demanded the judge.

"Lisabeth."

"Where are you?"

"I'm in the schoolroom. I've tried and tried to get out, but I'm locked in; and I've been here since all the afternoon," the voice wailed. Tears were not far away.

"What?" exclaimed the judge.

"Yes, sir, I came back to get my books; and the girls had all gone home, and I s'pose the janitor thought everybody was out and locked the outside door; and I banged and banged, but nobody heard me."

"Why didn't you call before?"

"I tried to, but couldn't make you hear, until I thought of the pointer."

"Well, well, well," said the judge. Then he lighted a match. "Lean out a bit and let me see you," he commanded. The yellow glare showed a pale little face with earnest blue eyes, red-rimmed from crying, and fair hair braided in a thick braid.

"Why haven't your people looked you up?" the old gentleman asked querulously, as the light went out.

"I haven't any people," sighed Lisabeth. "Only my sister."

"How old is she?"

"Oh, she'll soon be sixteen, and she works at Roby's ribbon counter. She won't get home till late tonight, 'cause they don't shut up until late on Christmas Eve."

"Hum," said the judge crustily. "I suppose I'll have to look after you."

He went back to his desk, and Lisabeth, shivering at the open window, saw him pick up the telephone receiver.

Suddenly he put it down and came back to the window.

"Are you hungry?" he asked.

"Awfully," said the little voice in the darkness.

"Why didn't you say so before?" questioned the judge testily. "Before I ate up my dinner?"

"I couldn't make you hear, you know," was the patient answer.

"Well, there's nothing left but some crackers and an orange."

"Oh, an orange!" Lisabeth's sigh was rapturous.

"Do you want them?"

"Oh, yes, thank you." Lisabeth wondered how the judge could ask such a question. But the judge had gone back to his desk, and was emptying the dish of crackers into a large manilla envelope. He laid the orange on top, pinned the flap, and tied a string around the whole.

"Reach over your pointer," he directed; and when Lisabeth had laid it across the chasm between the buildings, he hung the package upon it, and in another minute the little girl had drawn it over.

"Is it all right?" asked the judge, as he heard the crackle of the paper.

"Oh, yes, indeed! It is a delicious orange, perfectly delicious."

"Hmm," said the judge again, but this time there was just a ghost of a smile on his face as he went over to the telephone, called up police headquarters, and gave a peremptory order.

"They'll be up in a minute to let you out," he informed Lisabeth as he came back to the window. "And now I've got to get back to work, and you'd better shut the window."

"It's very dark," quavered the little voice.

Somewhere back in the judge's past there had been a little child who at night would say, "It is very dark, Father;

stay with me," and the judge had stayed, and had held the little clinging fingers until the child slept. But when the child grew to be a man, he had married a lady who did not please the judge, although she was sweet and good; but she was poor, and the judge was proud, and had hoped for greater things for his son. And so the son had gone away, and for years the old man had shut his heart to all tenderness; but now the little voice woke memories, so that the judge's tone was softer when he spoke again.

"Are you afraid?"

"It's dreadful lonesome," was the wistful answer, "and it's awfully nice to have you to talk to."

"Oh, is it?" said the flattered judge. "Well, you've got to wrap up if you stand there. It's freezing cold."

"Oh, I didn't think!" Lisabeth's tone was worried. "You will take cold. Oh, please shut your window."

But this the judge refused to do. "I'll put on my overcoat and pass Miss Jenkins's sweater over to you."

So while the important case waited for review, the two shrouded figures sat at opposite windows, while between them the snow came down faster and faster. The judge's office was brilliantly lighted, and Lisabeth could see every expression of the old man's face; but the judge could see nothing of the little girl, so that her voice seemed to come from out of the night.

❖

While they waited thus, Lisabeth told the judge about her older sister, who had taken care of them both ever since their father died, and how Lisabeth kept house when she was not at school; and, best of all, she told him that she had saved $1.25 to spend for Christmas presents, and she was going to buy a pair of gloves for sister.

"And what will you have for Christmas?" asked the judge, interested in spite of himself.

"Oh, sister'll give me something," said the child cheerfully. "Prob'ly it will be something useful. If she gives me a dress, she can't give me any toys or candy. And then, besides, she had to spend quite a bit for the dinner. Things are so 'spensive.

"You see," explained Lisabeth, "we're going to divide with the McGafneys on the top floor. They're awfully poor, and there's four children, but we're going to have pumpkin pie and lots of gravy and potatoes, so as to make enough. At first we thought we wouldn't ask them, and have enough ourselves for once; but sister decided that Christmas was the time to make other people happy, and of course it is."

"Of course," assented the judge, feeling very small indeed when he thought of his gruff reply to Miss Jenkins, and of how he had sent poor George away without even a Christmas wish.

On and on chatted the little voice in the darkness, while the judge, listening, felt the ice melt around his old heart.

"I shall have to eat my dinner all alone tomorrow," he found himself confiding, presently.

"Oh, you poor man!" cried the little girl. "Maybe we'll have enough—I'll ask my sister—" but before she could finish her invitation, a loud knock echoed through the building.

"They've come," said the judge. "Now you just sit still until they come upstairs and get you; don't go bumping around in the dark. I'll go down and see them." And out he rushed, leaving Lisabeth to face his lighted window alone.

The police having found the janitor, the door was quickly opened; the lights soon flared in the halls; and in a minute Lisabeth was surrounded by a little crowd composed of two jolly policemen, the janitor, and a half dozen people who had watched the opening of the door.

"You'd better take her straight to the station, Murphy," said one policeman to the other, "and they can send her home from there."

"You won't do anything of the kind," said a commanding voice; and the judge came in, panting from his climb up the steps, his shoulders powdered with snow, with all the dignity that belongs to a judge, so that the policemen at sight of him touched their caps and the straggler looked at him respectfully.

"Order a taxi, Murphy," he said; and in less time than it takes to tell it, Lisabeth found herself on the soft cushions, with the judge beside her.

"I'll take her, Judge, if you're too busy," said Murphy, with his hand on the taxi door.

But the judge had forgotten his important case. The clinging fingers, the look in the trustful blue eyes, made his old heart leap.

"Thank you, Murphy," he said. "I'll look after her. And oh, ah—a Merry Christmas, Murphy!" And he left the officer bewildered by the unusual kindliness of his tone.

As they rolled along, he pulled out his watch. "What time did you say your sister would get home?" he said.

"Not much before ten o'clock."

"It's only eight now," said the judge, "so I will get you something to eat. Then we will call for her."

The rest of the evening was a dream to the little girl. The wonderful dining room at the great hotel, where there were flowers and cut glass and silver on the lovely white tables, seemed just like fairyland.

When they were once more in the taxi, the judge ordered the driver to go to Roby's.

A crowd of girls streamed out from the doors of the

big store as they drove up, but Lisabeth made straight for a slender figure in a thin old coat. One of the girls called out.

"Marcella, Marcella Blair, wait a minute. Here's Lisabeth!"

Within the taxi the judge sat up straight and looked out at the sound of that name. She had called her "Marcella Blair," and he was Marcellus Blair!

Before Marcella could think or understand, they were in the taxi together, the sisters and an excited old gentleman, who kept asking questions: "Who was your father? How came you to be named Marcella?"

"After my grandfather," said the dazed Marcella. "He was Marcellus Blair."

And then the judge told her joyfully that he was Marcellus Blair and her grandfather, and—well, it was all so wonderful that Lisabeth simply sat speechless, and clasped her hands very tightly, and wondered if she was dreaming.

"And I have a letter from my father to you, sir," explained Marcella shyly. "He tried to find you after Mother's death. But you were abroad, and then . . . he died . . . and after that I did not know what to do."

"Why didn't you hunt me up?" demanded the judge. "Why didn't you hunt me up?"

"I tried to once," said Marcella, "but the city was so big—"

"Oh, oh," groaned the judge, "and all this time I have been so lonely!"

And then Lisabeth tucked her hand into his. "But you will never be lonely anymore, Grandfather," she said.

And he wasn't; for he took Marcella and Lisabeth home with him that very night, and the very next day the McGafneys had all of the dinner for themselves, and Marcella and Lisabeth ate in the judge's great dining room; and that night, as the happy three sat in the library in front of a roaring fire, Lisabeth laid her head on her grandfather's shoulder.

"It *was* lucky I was locked in, Grandfather," she said, "or you might not have found us."

But the judge, with one arm around her waist and the other reached out to Marcella, shook his head. "Don't talk of luck, dearie," he said. "It was something more than that; it was Providence."

Have You Seen the Star?

❋

MARGARET SLATTERY

*This turn-of-the-century story is as pow-
erful now as when it was first written. The
question, "Have you seen the star?" takes
on new meaning in Margaret Slattery's
story: not the mere visual experience, but a
much deeper, life-changing one.*

*The origins of the story are obscure;
however, one thing is certain: It deserves to
live on.*

Margaret Slattery's surviving sto-

ries are few, but those few I have ever seen are well worth the reading.

"Fourth floor, please." Mrs. Carston left the elevator and walked down the broad aisle between toy motor cars, toy rocking horses, dolls, and games. She stopped beside the rail which enclosed the square set apart for the children where attendants helped them into marvelous wings, lifted them to the backs of camels, elephants, or horses on the merry-go-round, or let them sail tiny boats on a miniature sea. The young woman stood fascinated. This would be the third year that she had spent a morning before that rail. The joyous laughter and those happy faces brought back the memories of her own little boy who was just five years old last month. It seemed cruel that the man who had been her husband should have this child at Christmas, yet she could not bear to think of the long summer days by the lake without his smiling face and the warm caress of his chubby hands. Three years it had been since the court had decided that father and mother might live apart but should share the boy for equal periods of six months.

Now he had the boy, and it was only a few days before Christmas.

Of course, her boy would not be there in a public playroom, but she liked to find the boys who resembled him. Watching them at their play, she suddenly realized that she was sobbing and laughing, then crying and laughing at the same time and not able to stop. A woman in a white uniform led her away to the Emergency Room where, after what seemed a long rest, the nurse asked if she had lost a child. The question revived her. Those people had no right to know. She said she felt better and ordered a taxi to take her home.

When she had taken off her wraps and thrown herself upon the couch, she told her faithful maid that she had become exhausted while in one of the stores and would have a light lunch served there in her room before trying to sleep. She half heard the words of sympathy, the scolding for doing too much, but the caress and the careful arrangement of pillows were a comfort. After the lunch, she tried in vain to sleep. Wandering about the room, her eyes fell on a little red book which she had thrown on the table a week before. A friend had persuaded her to attend a tabernacle service. At the close of the meeting, a young woman with a most attractive face had given her the little book, saying, "Will you not read it sometime, please?" She had smiled and had said, "Yes," but had not done it. Now she opened the little book, and lying down again, began to read the verses marked in red. Utterly worn out by the strain of the morning, she did not read long, but closing her eyes, thought over the words. The rain which had been threatening all day began to fall and the room grew dark. Turning her face toward the wall she finally slept.

In her dream she found herself mixed up with a large procession of every sort of people who were rushing along a great highway toward a soft gray curtain of cloud which hid the sky. Where it touched the earth, a man stood with a long robe and with a wonderful face. "Where are you all going?" she asked those by her side. A gray-haired woman responded, "To see the star. It is the Bethlehem star, you know. They say that if you can see it, your mind and heart will be at peace and you will be happy the rest of your life." The younger woman looked at the unhappy faces about her and then said, "I will walk along with you; we all look as though we need something to make us happy." After a long time, she found herself before the man with the wonderful face and his keen eyes looked her through. "Would you see the star?"

"Yes, I want peace of mind and heart. I need it."

"Will you pay? It is a costly star."

"What must I pay?" she asked fearfully.

"Will you try to forgive him?" he asked so softly that no one else could hear.

"Oh, not that," she cried. "Anything but that."

"It is that price you must pay to see the star and know its peace."

But she shook her head and slowly joined the company of disappointed seekers who were going down the hill. Tears filled her eyes as she stumbled along. On the great plain below, she saw men lying dead in the snow, hundreds of them, the smoke of burning cities and the blaze of bursting shells.

A voice seemed to say, "If only those who have brought men to this could see the star, peace would come to earth. But it is a costly star and they will not pay." Failing to locate the speaker, she walked on and after a long time sat down to rest. There at the foot of the hill was a brightly lighted home. Before the fireplace a man and woman stood facing each other with hate and anger deforming their faces. A moment more and the man flung himself furiously into his coat and left the house. Again the mysterious voice remarked, "They need to see the star, but they will not pay. Neither can put himself in the place of the other. See, see the scores of wrecked homes—little children in them suffering the penalty. Selfishness has made both men and women deaf and blind."

Scorched by the words which seemed to touch her inmost soul, she cried out, "Lead me back; I must go back; I must see the star."

"You called? Did you want anything? It sounded as if you were in pain." The maid stood at the door, anxious and troubled.

"No," she answered. "I must have dreamed. I am glad you wakened me. Frank and Louise are coming for dinner and I'll have to dress at once."

Contrary to her usual dread of spending an evening alone, she longed to have her friends leave soon that she might be able to think. When at last the good-nights had been said, she hurried to her room, undressed quickly, and turned on her bed lamp to read the Testament again. How many times she had read all night seeking to drown memories that would not let her sleep—but never words like these. She had never taken religion very seriously. The life of the one who began in that manger to which the thoughts of millions would turn on Christmas morning and ended in the day's agony on a cross, and the glory of the open tomb, had never before deeply impressed her. But now she closed the book and turned out the light, conscious of an unseen and sympathetic presence.

In the dark she began to think of the days when James Carston had told her that he loved her. Then her wedding, the first year in his father's home, the misunderstanding—then the baby. Crowding upon each other came the memories of the things which she had said to him the day the child was a year old—of the words of cold disdain with which he had met her storms of anger. "He should have been more patient," but now the words of the dream came hauntingly: "Neither can put himself in the other's place. Selfishness has made both men and women deaf and blind." Memories of the child came rushing over her—the last awful scene when the man had begged her to try again, to make one more attempt to understand him. He had said he would do anything to save them (for the child's sake) from the publicity of separation, but she had answered that she would never forgive him and that she would relieve him of the burden of both herself and the child. She had meant then to take her little two-year-old son and go back to her own home, but the court had said no. All their quarrels had started with such little things, but how the memories hurt! Forgive him? It was the price of the star! Then she would never see it. . . . The loneliness and longing would not be banished, for she could not fight it off with hard and bitter thoughts as before. Finally, in the gray light of early morning, she rose and knelt by the bed. After a long time she said slowly and aloud to the Presence, "Show me the star. I will pay. I will *try* to forgive him. I will forgive. Help me!" It was her first prayer. Into her heart came the sense of peace. Comforted and conscious of sustaining strength, she went back to bed. The stars were fading. One seemed brighter than the other, and watching it, she fell asleep.

While Alma Carston had been dressing for dinner and trying in vain to shake herself free from her dream, the man who had been her partner in what he often sarcastically called the disillusionment, sat in his living room with his little son upon his knee. The child had been saying a piece which he was to repeat with the other children at a Christmas service. With expression and accuracy that would have done credit to a person much older than just five, he said the words of the first Christmas story. His aunt had taught it to him carefully but refused to answer any questions about the things which she taught, and this evening a whole volley of them followed the recitation of the piece. Angels and wise men, shepherds and camels, mangers, gold, frankincense and myrrh, all came in for their share; and the questionnaire ended with three important questions: "Did you ever see the star, Daddy?" "Have you ever looked for it?" "Wouldn't you like to see it?"

Negative answers came from the man whose thoughts flew back over the years to the day when he himself stumbled through the words, "We have seen His star in the East and are come to worship Him."

The child soon changed the subject, and shaking the father by his shoulders, demanded, "Tell me, Daddy, am I going to have a Christmas tree? Am I?"

"Sure, sure you are. A big tree that will touch the ceiling this year since you are a big boy."

"What will be on it?"

"What do you want on it?"

The boy did not hesitate for a moment. He had evidently thought it over before. When breathless the boy finished, his father exclaimed, "One tree? You will need a forest of Christmas trees."

"Who is going to come to my tree, Daddy? The big cousins who came last year—will they come?"

"Yes, we'll ask anybody you want."

"Truly? Will we, Daddy?" He snuggled down into his

father's arms and played with the fingers of the hand that held him tightly.

He was silent so long that his father said, "Well, have you decided who you want?"

"Yes," the child answered, "I want Mother. Last Christmas she didn't have any tree. I asked her in the summer. She had only presents—she liked mine the best, but she didn't have any candy—nobody gave her any. Daddy, I wish you and Mother lived in the same house. Helen's daddy and her mother live in the same house, and so do Allen's," he sighed. "I asked Mother all summer to come and see us and she has never come. She's got lovely sunshine hair and she can swim fine. She taught me, only I can't do it yet." He was still a moment or two and then added, "I guess I'll ask Carl. He's a scout. That'll be enough. She can tell stories lots better than Auntie and better than you, Daddy. Maybe she'll tell one an—"

His aunt interrupted by saying that it was past time for bed and Daddy's dinner was ready. The child seldom spoke of his mother for he found that no one answered, and a strange uncomfortable feeling always followed the mention of her name, but having started talking about her, he found it very hard to stop and protested vigorously as his aunt led him away.

James Carston did not eat very heartily and he was

not in a talkative mood. "Sunshine hair." He had told her that very thing himself. He remembered the day on the lake and the look with which she answered him. And he had taught her to swim. She was so vigorous that she had soon surpassed her teacher.

Immediately after dinner, he left for the midweek service of the church in which he was an officer. When his father had died, the whole congregation had mourned the loss of their most prominent member and real friend, and they had persuaded him to take his father's place. Of late, he had often tried to give it up, but they would not listen to it. Usually he did not attend the weekly service, but tonight his presence had been requested, for over a hundred people were to seek membership in the church—the largest number that had ever come before it. James Carston paid little attention to the singing, none whatever to the prayer, though his head was bowed. He was lost in his own thoughts during the opening paragraph of the minister's talk but was brought back by the words, "Have you seen the star? You men and women of this city . . ." and his boy's question,

"Have you seen the star, Daddy?" The minister was certain that not many had seen it. He said that men today found it difficult to seek stars; they loved their own will and way, were filled with pride, were steeped in greed and selfishness. . . .

James Carston walked home that night alone. Ever since the day when the court, at the bidding of his influence, his money, and his demand, had given the boy into his keeping for the half year, the holidays had been a source of dread. As the child grew older, the strange arrangement of a mother in the summer and a father in the winter, and never both, puzzled him, and of late his questions were hard to answer. Someday the boy would have to be told. What should he tell him? What would she tell him? What poor reinforcement their example would be when it was his turn to meet life's temptations.

On the way to his own room, the father stopped to look at the boy. How often he stood gazing down at the child so like himself, wishing that he might always keep him a boy of five. Tonight he stood longer than usual, then went to bed to lie staring into the darkness, thinking of things that even his strong will could not banish. He did not know that within a half hour's walk she was struggling to forgive him that she might see the star.

In spite of all effort, now he remembered his taunting words when the court had given him his son, remembered the intolerant fashion in which during the first years he had dismissed her as unreasonable or laughed at her judgments. She was young, she had been the only daughter, unrestrained and petted, and he had not given her a long time to learn new ways. He felt a deep sense of shame for the first time. He gave up the fight against the memories and let them come . . . the night the boy was born . . . how courageous she had been . . . he felt for a moment that he would like to go to her and say that he had been unfair, but he had never said that to anyone. . . .

He did not see the child the next morning. It was raining, and as he stepped out into the chill air, he hated the world. Business was dull for him at the holidays and that afternoon his work was done at three o'clock. He sat looking out over the roofs of the city, thinking in spite of himself of the boy's wish that his mother come to the Christmas tree, of the sunshine hair and the stories. She would not come of course, but what should he say to the child by way of explanation? Why not send the boy to her for Christmas? The words darted into his consciousness as if they had been spoken aloud. That, he told himself, would never do, but the words of the minister the night before persistently penetrated his thinking.

It was a perfectly appointed office——his father's position, business, home, everything he had was his father's and yet he had never measured up as a boy or as a young man to what his father expected and hoped for him. His little son had his father's ways. He looked up at the picture of the keen, strong face of his father on his desk. Tears sprang to his eyes and yielding to a sudden overwhelming impulse, he bowed his head upon his desk and cried aloud, "Oh God, help me." He sat there a long time and then the MIRACLE came. . . . The Creator touched the soul of the man He had made and completed His creation. The words that were wrung from the awakened soul were those of a strong man yielding himself to a greater will: saying out of desperate struggle, "I will do right. . . . Thy will." The strengthening presence of a brother who had been through a man's Gethsemane stole into the office on the twelfth floor so quietly that the great noisy bustling city roared on unaware.

It was after five when he left his office. He had made his plans. He would send the child to her in the morning for the holidays and the tree would follow. When the boy was told, a shout of joy filled the house. "Oh Daddy, Daddy, couldn't we go now?" The "we" stung the heart of the man, who could not help the jealous pang that came as the boy clapped his hands and danced around the room.

Putting the child to bed that night was a difficult task for the boy's aunt, but she made no comment. When hours later James Carston looked in at him, the child stirred in his sleep, opened his eyes and, seeing his father, sat up quickly and cried, "Is it morning, Daddy?" The man shook his head, kissed the sleepy little face, and told him morning would come soon, and then hurried to his own room. Despite the wakeful hours and the morning that came too quickly, the man felt a strange quietness of mind and heart that he had never known before.

At eight o'clock they telephoned to ask if Mrs. Carston would be at home that morning. She would be there until eleven. At half past nine, his suitcase packed and dressed in the fur-trimmed coat that made him look, in his aunt's words, "perfectly adorable," the boy climbed into the motorcar with his father and a maid. The man began to give instructions to the half-listening child as to what he should say and do. "Tell your mother Daddy sent you for the holidays because you wanted her at your Christmas tree. The tree will come at noon. Tell her you are a Christmas visitor. You can stay until the New Year, then Mary will come for you. Listen Sonny, be sure and telephone Daddy every day at half past four. I'll be in the office Christmas Day, too. Don't forget."

The chauffeur was turning the car—there was the apartment. The man seized his son, holding him tightly, and kissed him again and again. He suddenly felt that the Divine

Will of the heavenly court might ask him to leave with the lonely woman the child who loved her and wanted her. Somehow it seemed too much. . . .

Not until the maid picked up the suitcase did the boy realize that his father was not going in with him. He stood still on the walk. "Aren't you coming, Daddy?" and in response to his father's no, the little face shadowed. "Is it going to be like summer?" he asked sadly. The man could hardly answer. "Run along, Laddie," he said. "You're a Christmas surprise. Think how surprised she'll be. I will send the tree at noon." He watched them enter the big door of the great modern apartment then rapidly walked away, conscious of a Presence which calmed his soul.

Alma Carston was writing a list of names when the bell rang. The day before had been the first in years that she had known peace, or even approached happiness. The list of names included old friends whom she had long neglected, lovers of books to whom she could deliver her gifts on Christmas morning; then she planned to go to church—

she had not been there on Christmas Day since she was a little girl.

With every thought of dread of the day came the soothing memory of the star that she had paid to see. Not hearing the doorbell, she was astonished to hear the exclamation of her maid and then a child's laugh. A moment later found her in the hall. The surprise was almost too much but she heard it saying, "Daddy sent me. I'm a Christmas visitor, a surprise, and the tree will come at noon 'cause I wanted you for my Christmas tree." Had it not been for the child's evident joy and his insistence that the suitcase be unpacked, his questions about where they should put the tree, what should be on it, whether Carl the scout might come to it—a perfect volley of questions that gave her no time to think—she could not have controlled the emotions that surged over her. At noon, as they sat down for lunch at the little table she always used for him at the lake, he looked over at her, his face beaming, and said, "It's nice isn't it, Mother. Just like summer only it's almost Christmas." She could keep back the tears no longer and fled to her room, but he followed her, calling, "Has it come? Has the tree come? Daddy said it would." And it had. It must be attended to and there was no time for tears when a Christmas tree had to be looked after. A box filled with all sorts of decorations came with the tree and it was nearly four o'clock when tinsel and gay balls, colored chains of every sort, candles that must be lighted, Santa Clauses little and big, and a wonderful electric star were fastened to the branches to the satisfaction of both the decorators.

The child was tired and content to lie quietly in his mother's arms listening to "The Night Before Christmas." "Tell it to me, Mother," he begged. "Daddy doesn't know it and Auntie doesn't say it like you do. . . ."

Two or three times he had said, "Is it half past four?" and as the story closed he asked again. "Why do you want to know, darling?" she asked. "Cause then every day I telephone Daddy. I mustn't forget it," he answered. "It's half past four now," she said and he ran to the telephone. He seemed such a baby to her that she listened in astonishment as the clear little voice gave the correct number. She did not know how often he had interrupted important business interviews since he had learned the call.

"Hello, Daddy. It's come. Yes. She was very surprised. It's all decorated. Yes, it's beautiful. . . . I like it. . . . There aren't any presents on it but there will be in the morning. . . . Yes, lots and lots." Then, in dismay she heard him pleading, "Daddy, won't you come and see it 'fore I go to bed? We can light the star when it's dark. Will you come? No, Daddy, tonight. What?" And then he turned to his mother. "He says, Can he come to see it and I said I'd ask you. Can he, Mother? Say yes, quick. . . . You can, Daddy; I asked her nice and she says you can." The man at the other end of the wire tried to speak calmly but the child said, "I can't hear you, Daddy—what? Then all right, good-bye. He'll come at half past six," he announced. "Oh, Mother, aren't we glad?"

The woman, leaning her head upon her hands, did not know what to answer. The child looked at her with misgivings as she said cheerfully, "My little boy must take a nap right away. I'll wake you at six and then we can be ready when Daddy comes." The small arms clasped tightly about her neck, the warm kisses of the boy who from babyhood had been an unusually affectionate child, seemed so good to her after the long months that she lay beside him thinking of what it would mean if she need never let him go again. The arms relaxed and, turning on his side, the child slept quietly. She watched him pressing one soft little hand again and again to her lips. "I will tell him I have paid to see the star. I do forgive him. Do you hear me, my boy?" But the child did not hear.

She did not need to waken him, for in less than an hour he sat up rubbing his eyes. "Has Daddy come? Can we light the star? It's dark enough, isn't it?"

He sprang out of bed to be made ready. The bell

rang—it was only the last mail—very late. Again, but it was a box of flowers from a friend. Then a third time, and she heard her maid's cold and dignified greeting. The boy ran to his father, but the father scarcely saw him. He looked past the child at her—the first time he had seen her for three years. There was a new wonderful light in her face. He had planned carefully what he should say to her about their being friends for the sake of the boy, but instead of the carefully chosen words he cried passionately, "Try to forgive me," and reached out both arms to her. She looked into his face and saw there what all the years had never shown her. She did not know that he had only just found his soul, but she knew in a moment that she wanted, longed to forgive and be forgiven.

"I do, I do," she responded and went to him. Those moments seemed to blot out the pain of years.

The child stood waiting, puzzled at the scene which did not please him. Suddenly, in a trembling voice, he protested. "Come, Mother, let's show him the tree. Daddy, just look at the star—it is lighted." But the man and woman who followed their son into the room where the tree glistened had seen another Star in whose light selfishness died, a costly star that brought reconciliation and peace, a star that all the men and women and nations of the world may see if they will pay the price.

Yet Not One of Them Shall fall . . .

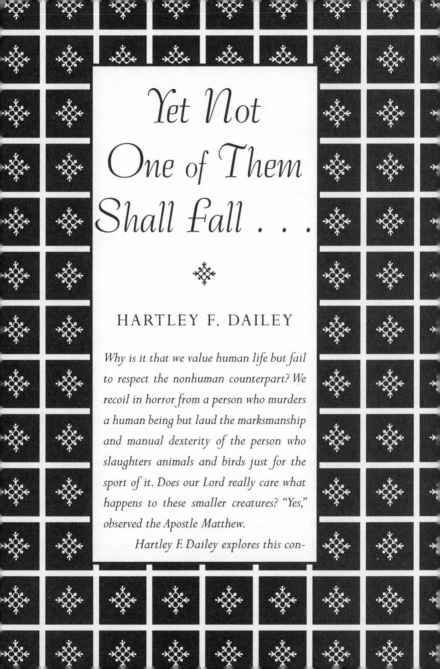

HARTLEY F. DAILEY

Why is it that we value human life but fail to respect the nonhuman counterpart? We recoil in horror from a person who murders a human being but laud the marksmanship and manual dexterity of the person who slaughters animals and birds just for the sport of it. Does our Lord really care what happens to these smaller creatures? "Yes," observed the Apostle Matthew.

Hartley F. Dailey explores this con-

cept in this poignant narrative. Even though this story is not in-cluded in the four Gospels, Dailey feels it would be in character for it to have actually happened, especially in light of the Apostle John's concluding words:

> *But there are also many other things which Jesus did;*
> *were every one of them to be written, I suppose that the*
> *world itself could not contain the books that would be*
> *written. (John 21:25)*

All day the sky had hung leaden and threatening over the "City of David," the sleepy little town of Bethlehem. It was the time of the rains, but no rain was falling, neither rain nor snow had thus far blessed the fields and groves round about. The countryside lay parched and dry, shivering be-neath an unnatural northeast wind which should not be blowing at this season at all.

Travelers poured into the town in unwonted num-bers, for it was the time of the great census, when every man was ordered to journey to the place of his tribe to be counted. Camels, donkeys, oxen, and the tramp of human feet had ground the dry soil of the streets into dust. It lay ankle-deep in the streets, it powdered the garments of travelers, it choked the throats and stung the eyes. It crept through the carefully shuttered windows of the houses, and lay like a pall on the furnishings within.

Here and there through the streets a group of ruffian boys wandered, six or seven untidy, unmannerly fellows, the despair alike of their parents and the village elders. Lazy, impudent and self-willed, they seldom worked, they stayed away from school, they hung about all day on the streets causing trouble, making disrespectful remarks about passersby—in short, being generally obnoxious. Their ringleader was one Benjamin, son of Jonas, the prize miscreant of the lot, a rough ungainly lad of some fourteen summers. His father, a man of considerable consequence in the town, tried in vain to control his unruly son.

Today, Benjamin had proposed a game. Each boy bore a sling, two leather thongs with a pouch between, and a bag of small round stones. As they went along the street, one would pick out a target, and challenge some other of the group to hit it. This might be something small and difficult to hit, or again, it might be something considered very daring, as a bronze kettle hanging in the stall of Jonah, the merchant, or a fancy white donkey belonging to some rich caravan owner.

Suddenly, one in the group called out, "Look there, Benjamin, across the street, on the corner of old Eli's house, bet you can't hit that from here!"

Contemptuously, the young ruffian fitted a stone in his sling. He sneered as he drew back his arm. "Ha," he boasted. "By the beard of Abraham, I don't even need both eyes to sling at that! I could hit such a mark with one eye closed!" Expertly, he swung the sling three times around his head, and let fly the stone.

His boast wasn't idle. The stone sped straight and true, and though the little sparrow he had aimed at started to fly, it was too late. The stone struck it upon the wing. Its intended flight turned into a helpless flutter, and it went spinning down into the alley between the houses. The boys didn't even bother to go look at it, or end its misery with a merciful death. They cheered their leader and slapped his back, then, noting the approach of Eli, who was no friend of theirs, drifted away in search of other mischief.

But the bird was not without a friend: Simon, the little hunchback orphan boy, was searching up and down the alleys, hoping to find a scrap of food, or a useful bit of rag to add to his pitiful clothing. He didn't dare show himself to the other boys. His ugly misshapen form made him the butt of their jokes—and worse. His arms, as a result of his infirmity, were so weak he was incapable of defending himself. But as the miscreants moved away, he crept to the mouth of the alley, and gathered the sparrow up in his hands.

At first, it struggled wildly. Simon could feel the terrified beating of its timid heart, as his hands gently stroked it, smoothing the injured wing against its side, doing his best to put the broken bone in place. Gradually, its struggles subsided till finally it snuggled down between his warming hands with a contented little chirp. Then Simon made a place for it in the bosom of the filthy rag he called his cloak, and went on with his search.

Life was hard. Disfigured from birth, he was shunned by most of the village because of his repulsive looks. Many actively hated him, for one in his condition was supposed to bring some kind of bad luck. More often than not when he asked for alms, he received blows and curses instead. He had never seen his father. When his mother died, two years ago, he had lost his last friend. The very condition which made it impossible for him to earn a living turned away those who might have helped him.

As evening came on, he made his way toward the caravans at the edge of town. The cook at the inn there was a rough, hard-handed man with a heart of gold. Sometimes, if there was no one to interfere, he would allow Simon to turn the roasting spit. Later, he would give the boy scraps of food left by the guests. Comforts were few in Simon's life. To sit in the glow of heat from the charcoal cooking fire, to smell the delicious odors of the roasting meat, these were the finest experiences he knew, and the scraps of bone and fat discarded by the guests at the inn were his most nourishing food.

But tonight was not his lucky night. Some great Roman was stopping at the inn, and he had sent his slave to the kitchen to oversee the preparation of his food. When that worthy caught sight of Simon, he flew into a rage.

"Out, out, you misbegotten swine!" he shouted. "No filthy offal such as you shall hang around the kitchen where my master's food is cooked. Get out, before I throw your filthy carcass to the dogs!"

Disconsolate, Simon turned away. But the rough old cook, pretending to hurry him out, slipped a hard chunk of bread into his hand. Once outside, the boy sat down in the stable yard to eat his bread. Since he had tasted hardly a bite of food all day, even the hard dry bread tasted good. But, hungry as he was, he broke off a portion and fed it to the bird, crumb by crumb.

Later, he made his way to the stable built into the hillside behind the inn. Here were stabled the cow and donkey belonging to the innkeeper, as well as the mounts of a few more affluent travelers. Here also, in a little stall at one end, were kept a few fat sheep, waiting to be slaughtered for the inn table. Simon had often slept among them. They were gentle beasts, and their soft, woolly sides were a fine bulwark against the chill of the night; soon, his head resting on the side of one of them, he was fast asleep.

Late in the night, he was awakened by a commotion such as he had seldom heard before. A long time he lay very still, terrified that the sounds might be made by robbers attacking the caravan outside, and the attempts of the owners to drive them off. But at last, within the very stable walls, he heard the plaintive cry of a small baby. Simon could contain himself no longer: He rose to his knees, and peered between the vertical bars which separated the sheep pen from the rest of the stable. He gazed in amazement on the scene there, then rubbed his eyes to see if he were dreaming.

Seated upon a robe atop a pile of hay, a Mother held an obviously newborn baby in her lap. Gathered before her in attitudes of worship were a group of shepherds—but, more remarkable, three richly clad strangers were kneeling right there upon the dirty stable floor, and presenting costly gifts to this baby; this baby who could not have been more than a couple of hours old.

The boy watched in awe. Never had he seen such men

137

as these, even in this town astride the caravan route from the East. And to find them here, kneeling in the stable dirt! A strange feeling crept over him. Who was this child, that these rich men should bow before him, and give him gold and other precious things? For some unexplainable reason, he wished that he might do the same.

Almost without willing it, Simon had climbed the stable bars. He thoroughly expected to be driven from the stable with blows and curses. But a roughly dressed man— he must have been the baby's father—took his hand then led him toward the child; and the rich men moved aside to let him pass, as though he had been a very prince. So presently he found himself kneeling there, in the forefront of all those gathered before the babe.

"My Lord," he stammered. "Dear little baby, I, too, would give thee a gift. But I am only an orphan and a cripple. The only thing I have to give is the little bird I found today." He took the sparrow tenderly from inside his cloak, and held it out before him.

The Mother turned the Child so that he faced Simon, and the baby suddenly opened his eyes, so that his gaze seemed to rest squarely upon the wounded bird. The sparrow seemed to shudder, and then suddenly it spread its wings, one of which had certainly been broken only a moment before, and soared into the air. Three times it circled over the heads of the transfixed watchers, then briefly hovered above the Mother and Child.

Simon knelt there trembling in nervous fear and awe. Then he saw that the strange dark eyes were looking at him. Without knowing why, he felt compelled to return that gaze. He felt as if he were drowning, or falling into the bottomless pit of that fathomless gaze. There was a feeling of fiery force which seemed to flow throughout his body, then he felt turned and twisted in some way he could not understand. There was a moment of almost unbearable pain, and then he was rising to his feet.

For a moment Simon could not understand what had happened: Things looked so different! It came to him that never before had he looked upon the world from this height, or from this angle. His arms had never seemed so straight, nor felt so strong. And the man who had led him in was kneeling on the floor praying, his eyes lifted Heavenward.

"Hear, O Israel," he prayed. "The Lord they God, He is one God. Praise to Thee, O Lord, for this night have I seen Thy work begun!" Suddenly, realization came to the boy. He no longer was a hunchback.

The father of the Child came suddenly to lay a hand upon his head. "My Son," he said, "tonight you have been given a new back. Such miracles are not wasted. I do not know how, but someday, when this babe has become a man, he will have need of that back. When that time comes, though you have roamed to the very end of the earth, you will be there beside him. By what name are you called, and whence came you?"

"I am Simon, Sir," the lad replied, "an orphan. My father was the leader of a mighty caravan. But he was killed by robbers in the year that I was born. He used to live in Cyrene, before he came here and met my mother. I think that I shall go there, now that I am whole and strong. Perhaps some of my father's people are living there still."

So saying, he turned away, and went out into the first light of morning.

(In the Gospel according to Matthew, we read, "Are not two sparrows sold for a farthing? Yet not one of them shall fall to the ground unless your Father wills it." Matthew 10:29)

Mr. Sankey Celebrates Christmas

✻

JOHN GILLIES

It's a long arm that stretches from guard duty near Sharpsburg, Maryland, during the Civil War to a Pennsylvania riverboat in 1875. It's almost eerie to witness such a graphic example of God's incredible choreography.

The stocky, mustachioed man nervously paced the deck of a Delaware River steamer, unbuttoning his frock coat, and regularly removing his derby to wipe his brow. He looked much older than his thirty-five years.

It was unseasonably warm for a Christmas Eve.

The man stared at the passing Pennsylvania shoreline, thinking of his family in Newcastle, some three hundred miles to the West, whom he might not see this Christmas, unless he made his train connection in Philadelphia. Christmas, 1875.

"Pardon me, sir. Aren't you Ira Sankey, the gospel singer?"

He smiled at the lady and her husband. He assumed the man was her husband. He thought he was gracious to acknowledge that he was, indeed, Ira D. Sankey.

"We've seen your pictures in the newspapers."

He had not wanted to be recognized: Not today, not tonight. He was tired and fretful and warm. Fact of the matter was, he was angry and provoked with Mr. Moody.

"We thought you were still in England!" said the lady.

"We returned last week, madam," Mr. Sankey replied in his resonant baritone voice. And if Mr. Moody hadn't insisted on more conferences and meetings, he thought, he would have been home by now for Christmas with his family. Instead he was a prisoner on a river steamer.

"Mr. Sankey, would you sing for us? It is Christmas Eve. And we'd love to hear you."

Mr. Sankey said he would sing, and his presence was announced loudly across the deck. As the people gathered, he pondered what he might sing. He wished he had his portable pump organ, which had become an integral counterpart to his singing. But no matter. He would sing a Christmas carol or two, unaccompanied. Perhaps he would get the passengers to sing along with him.

He tried to shed his melancholy. He was a famous person, whether he liked it or not, and he was not normally shy about his gifts. He was known on two continents as the gospel singer, the song leader and soloist working with Dwight L. Moody, who was surely the greatest evangelist of the day. Perhaps God had intended it this way—for him to be in this place, on this boat, at this particular time.

"I thought I would sing a carol or two." Then, he added, "But somehow I feel I should sing another song."

"Sing one of your own songs!" shouted someone unseen. "Sing 'The Ninety-and-Nine!' " commanded another.

"No, thank you very much, but I now know what I must sing." He was smiling broadly now, feeling much bet-

❖

ter about himself and this situation, enjoying his congregation. "I shall sing a song by William Bradbury. And if you know it, as I'm sure many of you do, hum along with me."

Sankey began "Savior, Like a Shepherd, Lead Us."

> *Much we need Thy tenderest care.*
> *In Thy pleasant pastures feed us*
> *For our use Thy folds prepare.*
> *Blessed Jesus, Blessed Jesus,*
> *Thou has bought us, Thine we are.*

He sang all three verses. There was uncommon silence and Ira Sankey felt it would be inappropriate to sing anything else. So he simply wished everyone a Merry Christmas and the people murmured a greeting in return. The silence returned and he was alone.

"Your name is Ira Sankey?"

"Yes." He recognized neither the voice nor the man.

The man came out of the shadows. He was about his own age, with a beard beginning to turn gray, and comfortably but not fastidiously dressed. Perhaps he was in sales, a traveling man.

"Were you ever in the army, Mr. Sankey?"

"Yes, I was. I joined up in 1860."

"I wonder if you can remember back to 1862. Did you ever do guard duty, at night, in Maryland?"

"Yes, I did!" Sankey felt a stab of memory and excitement. "It might have been at Sharpsburg."

"I was in the army, too. The Confederate army. And I saw you that night."

Sankey looked at him warily.

"You were parading in your blue uniform. Had you in my sights, you standing there in the light of the full moon, which was right foolish of you, you know." The man paused. "Then you began to sing."

Amazingly, Sankey remembered.

"You sang the same song you sang tonight. 'Savior, Like a Shepherd, Lead Us.' "

"I remember."

"My mother sang that song a lot but I never expected no soldier to be singing it at midnight, on guard duty. Especially a Union soldier." The man sighed. "Obviously I didn't shoot you."

"And obviously I am grateful," Sankey smiled.

"I always wondered who you were. Who it was I didn't kill that night, on account of his singing an old Sunday school song."

Sankey just shook his head.

"Frankly, up until tonight, the name of Ira Sankey wouldn't have meant much to me. Guess I don't read the paper like I should. I didn't know you'd turn out to be so famous!" The man smiled for the first time. "But I reckon I would have recognized the voice and the song anyplace."

Sankey reflected on what might have been.

"Do you think we could talk a mite?" asked the man. "I think you owe it to me. Very little has gone right for me. Not before the war. Not during it. And not since."

Ira Sankey put an arm around his former enemy. They found a place in a quiet corner of the deck to sit and chat. Sankey's impatience and anger had passed. He no longer fretted that he might be delayed in seeing his family. Christmas would soon be here. It always came but sometimes in the strangest ways.

The night was still warm but it seemed filled with brighter stars.

Sankey even thought he heard the sound of angels' voices: singing, of course, and singing the Good News.

On Christmas Day in the Morning

❄

GRACE RICHMOND

Guy was upset—well, more than upset. Of all the grown Fernald family (Oliver, Edson, Ralph, Guy, Carolyn, and Nan), only Guy had gone home for Christmas. And even he had merely popped in for a few hours.

Next Christmas, he argued, should be better. But convincing all five to leave spouses and children and sneak into the old house as if they were kids again— well, that proved to be an uphill battle.

As for Guy, he didn't have a wife. And it was looking more and more like he never would.

I found it not long ago in a St. George, Utah, antique store. On seeing it, I did a double take, then a triple take, not believing my eyes. But there it was: undeniably a Christmas book by one of my all-time favorite authors, Grace Richmond (1866–1959). I was but a child when I first fell in love with her—and then the years have but deepened that attachment. I have savored her books, doling them out to read with the stinginess of a miser lest I complete her canon at too young an age. During the teens and twenties, Richmond was one of the most popular, and highest-paid, authors in America. Her books are beloved still (by a small but discerning audience); books such as The Twenty-Fourth of June, Cherry Square, Foursquare, Lights Up, Strawberry Acres, *and the very popular Red Pepper books.*

Since legendary Ladies' Home Journal *editor Edward Bok was a devotee of hers, I had seen Richmond's books serialized, and even some of her stories featured in old magazines, but never a Christmas story until this day. I would have paid almost anything the proprietor asked for it: I just knew it would be good!*

It was, and is. Actually, the book features two related stories about the same family, "On Christmas Day in the Morning" and a second (almost twice as long), "On Christmas Day in the Evening"—two of the finest things she ever wrote.

In fact, no archaeologist could possibly be more excited over this find than I.

> *And all the angels in heaven do sing,*
> *On Christmas Day, on Christmas Day;*
> *And all the bells on earth do ring,*
> *On Christmas Day in the morning.*
> *—Traditional.*

That Christmas Day virtually began a whole year beforehand, with a red-hot letter written by Guy Fernald to his younger sister, Nan, who had been married to Samuel Burnett just two and one half years. The letter was read aloud by Mrs. Burnett to her husband at the breakfast table, the second day after Christmas. From start to finish it was upon one subject, and it read as follows:

Dear Nan:

*It's a confounded, full-grown shame that not a
soul of us all got home for Christmas—except
yours truly, and he only for a couple of hours. What
have the blessed old folks done to us that we treat
them like this? I was invited to the Sewalls' for the
day, and went, of course—you know why. We had a
ripping time, but along toward evening I began to
feel worried. I really thought Ralph was home—he
wrote me that he might swing round that way by the
holidays—but I knew the rest of you were all wrapped
up in your own Christmas trees and weren't going to
get there.*

*Well, I took the seven-thirty down and walked
in on them. Sitting all alone by the fire, by George,
just like the pictures you see of "The Birds All Flown,"
and that sort of thing. I felt gulpish in my throat, on
my honor I did, when I looked at them. Mother just
gave one gasp and flew into my arms, and Dad got up
more slowly—his rheumatism is worse than ever this
winter—and came over and I thought he'd shake my
hand off. Well, I sat down between them by the fire,
and pretty soon I got down in the old way on a
cushion by mother, and let her run her fingers through
my hair, the way she used to—and Nan, I'll be*

indicted for perjury if her hand wasn't trembly. They were so glad to see me it made my throat ache.

Ralph had written he couldn't get round, and of course you'd all written and sent them things—jolly things, and they appreciated them. But—blame it all—they were just dead lonesome—and the whole outfit of us within three hundred miles, most within thirty!

Nan, next Christmas it's going to be different. That's all I say. I've got it all planned out. The idea popped into my head when I came away last night. Not that they had a word of blame—not they. They understood all about the children, and the cold snap, and Ed's being under the weather, and Oliver's wife's neuralgia, and Ralph's girl in the West, and all that. But that didn't make the thing any easier for them. As I say, next year—But you'll all hear from me then. Meanwhile, run down and see them once or twice this winter, will you, Nan? Somehow it struck me they aren't so young as—they used to be.

Splendid winter weather. Margaret Sewall's a peach, but I don't seem to make much headway. My best to Sam.

Your affectionate brother,

Guy

Sunny Nan had felt a slight choking in her own throat as she read this letter. "We really must make an effort to be there Christmas next year, Sam," she said to her husband, and Sam assented cheerfully. He only wished there were a father and mother somewhere in the world for him to go home to.

Guy wrote the same sort of thing, with more or less detail, to Edson and Oliver, his married elder brothers; to Ralph, his unmarried brother; and to Carolyn—Mrs. Charles Wetmore, his other, and elder, married sister. He received varied and more or less sympathetic responses, to the effect that with so many little children, and such snow-drifts as always blocked the roads leading toward North Es-tabrook, it really was not strange—and of course some-body would go next year. But they had all sent the nicest gifts they could find. Didn't Guy think mother liked those beautiful Russian sables Ralph sent her? And wasn't father pleased with his gold-headed cane from Oliver? Surely with such presents pouring in from all the children, Father and Mother Fernald couldn't feel so awfully neglected.

"Gold-headed cane be hanged!" Guy exploded when he read this last sentence from the letter of Marian, Oliver's wife. "I'll bet she put him up to it. If anybody dares give me a gold-headed cane before I'm ninety-five I'll thrash him with it on the spot. He wasn't using it, either—

bless him. He had his old hickory stick, and he wouldn't have had that if that abominable rheumatism hadn't gripped him so hard. He isn't old enough to use a cane, by jolly, and Ol ought to know it, if Marian doesn't. I'm glad I sent him that typewriter. He liked that, I know he did, and it'll amuse him, too—not make him think he's ready to die!"

Guy was not the fellow to forget anything which had taken hold of him as that pathetic Christmas homecoming had done. When the year had nearly rolled around, the first of December saw him at work getting his plans in train. He began with his eldest brother, Oliver, because he considered Mrs. Oliver the hardest proposition he had to tackle in the carrying out of his idea.

"You see," he expounded patiently, as they sat and stared at him, "it isn't that they aren't always awfully glad to see the whole outfit, children and all, but it just struck me it would do 'em a lot of good to revive old times. I thought if we could make it just as much as possible like one of the old Christmases before anybody got married—hang up the stockings and all, you know—it would give them a mighty jolly surprise. I plan to have us all creep in in the night and go to bed in our old rooms. And then in the morning . . . See?"

Mrs. Oliver looked at him. An eager flush lit his still boyish face—Guy was twenty-eight—and his blue eyes were very bright. His lithe, muscular figure bent toward her pleadingly; all his arguments were aimed at her. Oliver sat back in his impassive way and watched them both. It could not be denied that it was Marian's decisions which usually ruled in matters of this sort.

"It seems to me a very strange plan," was Mrs. Oliver's comment, when Guy had laid the whole thing before her in the most tactful manner he could command. She spoke rather coldly. "It is not usual to think that families should be broken up like this on Christmas Day, of all days in the year. Four families, with somebody gone—a mother or a father—just to please two elderly people who expect nothing of the sort, and who understand just why we can't all get home at once. Don't you think you are really asking a good deal?"

Guy kept his temper, though it was hard work. "It doesn't seem to me I am," he answered quite gently. "It's only for once. I really don't think father and mother would care much what sort of presents we brought them, if we only came ourselves. Of course, I know I'm asking a sacrifice of each family, and it may seem almost an insult not to invite the children and all, yet—perhaps next year we'll try a gathering of all the clans. But just for this year, honestly, I do awfully wish you'd give me my way. If you'd seen those two last Christmas—"

He broke off, glancing appealingly at Oliver himself. To his surprise, that gentleman shifted his pipe to the corner of his mouth and put a few pertinent questions to his younger brother. Had he thought it all out? What time should they arrive there? How early on the day after Christmas could they get away? Was he positive they could all crowd into the house without rousing and alarming the pair?

"Sure thing," Guy declared, quickly. "Marietta—well, you know I've had the soft side of her old heart ever since I was born, somehow. I talked it all over with her last year, and I'm solid with her, all right. She'll work the game. You see, father's quite a bit deaf now—"

"Father deaf?"

"Sure. Didn't you know it?"

"Forgotten. But mother'd hear us."

"No, she wouldn't. Don't you know how she trusts everything about the house to Marietta since she got that fall—"

"Mother get a fall?"

"Why, *yes!*" Guy stared at his brother with some impatience. "Don't you remember she fell down the back stairs a year ago last October and hurt her knee?"

"Certainly, Oliver," his wife interposed. "I wrote for you to tell her how sorry we were. But I supposed she had entirely recovered."

"She's a little bit lame, and always will be," said Guy, a touch of reproach in his tone. "Her knee stiffens up in the night, and she doesn't get up and go prowling about at the least noise, the way she used to. Marietta won't let her. So if we make a whisper of noise Marietta'll tell her it's the cat or something. No question at all! It can be worked all right. The only thing that worries me is the fear that I can't get you all to take hold of the scheme. On my word, Ol,"—he turned quite away from his sister-in-law's critical gaze and faced his brother with something like indignation in his frank young eyes—"don't we owe the old home anything but a present tied up in tissue paper once a year?"

Marian began to speak. She thought Guy was exceeding his rights in talking as if they had been at fault. It was not often that elderly people had so many children within call—loyal children who would do anything within reason. But certainly a man owed something to his own family. And at Christmas! Why not carry out this plan at some other—

Her husband abruptly interrupted her. He took his pipe quite out of his mouth and spoke decidedly.

"Guy, I believe you're right. I'll be sorry to desert my own kids, of course, but I rather think they can stand it for once. If the others fall into line, you may count on me."

Guy got away, feeling that the worst of his troubles was over. In his younger sister, Nan, he hoped to find an

160

ardent ally and he was not disappointed. Carolyn—Mrs. Charles Wetmore—also fell in heartily with the plan. Ralph, from somewhere in the far West, wrote that he would get home or break a leg. Edson thought the idea rather a foolish one, but was persuaded by Jessica, his wife, whom Guy privately declared a trump, that he must go by all means. And so they all fell into line, and there remained for Guy only the working out of the details.

"Mis' Fernald"—Marietta Cooley strove with all the decision of which she was capable to keep her high-pitched, middle-aged voice in order—" 'fore you get to bed I'm most forgettin' what I was to ask you. I s'pose you'll laugh, but Guy—he wrote me partic'lar he wanted you and his father to"—Marietta's rather stern, thin face took on a curious expression "to hang up your stockin's."

Mrs. Fernald paused in the doorway of the bedroom opening from the sitting room downstairs. She looked back at Marietta with her gentle smile.

"Guy wrote that?" she asked. "Then, it almost looks as if he might be coming himself, doesn't it, Marietta?"

"Well, I don't know's I'd really expect him," Marietta replied, turning her face away and busying herself about the hearth. "I guess what he meant was more in the way of a surprise for a Christmas present—something that'll go into a stockin', maybe."

"It's rather odd he should have written you to ask me," mused Mrs. Fernald, as she looked for the stockings.

Marietta considered rapidly. "Well, I s'pose he intended for me to get 'em on the sly without mentionin' it to you, an' put in what he sent, but I sort of guessed you might like to fall in with his idee by hangin' 'em up yourself, here by the chimbley, where the children all used to do it. Here's the nails, same as they always was."

Mrs. Fernald found the stockings, and touched her husband on the shoulder, as he sat unlacing his shoes. "Father, Guy wrote he wanted us to hang up our stockings," she said, raising her voice a little and speaking very distinctly. The elderly man beside her looked up, smiling.

"Well, well," he said, "anything to please the boy. It doesn't seem more than a year since he was a little fellow hanging up his own stocking, does it, Mother?"

The stockings were hung in silence. They looked thin and lonely as they dangled beside the dying fire. Marietta hastened to make them less lonely. "Well," she said, in a shamefaced way, "the silly boy said I was to hang mine, too. Goodness knows what he'll find to put into it that'll fit, 'less it's a poker."

They smiled kindly at her, wished her good night, and went back into their own room. The little episode had aroused no suspicions. It was very like Guy's affectionate boyishness.

"I presume he'll be down," said Mrs. Fernald, as she limped quietly about the room, making ready for bed. "Don't you remember how he surprised us last year? I'm sorry the others can't come. Of course, I sent them all the invitation, just as usual—I shall always do that—but it *is* pretty snowy weather, and I suppose they don't quite like to risk it."

Presently, as she was putting out the light, she heard Marietta at the door.

"Mis' Fernald, Peter Piper's got back in this part o' the house, somehow, and I can't lay hands on him. Beats me how cute that cat is. Seem's if he knows when I'm goin' to put him out in the wood shed. I don't think likely he'll do no harm, but I thought I'd tell you, so 'f you heard any queer noises in the night you'd know it was Peter."

"Very well, Marietta," the soft voice came back to the schemer on the other side of the door. "Peter will be all right, wherever he is. I shan't be alarmed if I hear him."

"All right, Mis' Fernald; I just thought I'd let you know," and the guileful one went grinning away.

There was a long silence in the quiet sleeping room. Then, out of the darkness, came this little colloquy:

"Emeline, you aren't getting to sleep."

"I know I'm not, John. I—Christmas Eve keeps one awake, somehow. It always did."

"Yes. . . . I don't suppose the children realize at all, do they?"

"Oh, no! Oh, no! They don't realize. They never will, till . . . they're here themselves. It's all right. I think—I think at least Guy will be down tomorrow, don't you?"

"I guess maybe he will." Then, after a short silence. "Mother, you've got me, you know. You know you've always got me, dear."

"Yes." She would not let him hear the sob in her voice. She crept close, and spoke cheerfully in his best ear. "And you've got me, Johnny Boy!"

"Thank the Lord, I have!"

So, counting their blessings, they fell asleep at last. But, even in sleep, one set of lashes was strangely wet.

"My goodness, what a drift!"

"Lucky we weren't two hours later."

"Sh-h—they might hear us."

"Nan, stop laughing, or I'll drop a snowball down your neck!"

"Here, Carol, give me your hand. I'll plough you through. Large bodies move slowly, of course, but go elbows first and you'll get there."

"Gee *whiz!* Can't you get that door open? I'll bet it's frozen fast."

A light showed inside the kitchen. The storm door swung open, propelled by force from inside. A cautious voice said low: "That the Fernald family?"

A chorus of whispers came back at Miss Marietta Cooley:

"Yes, yes—let us in, we're freezing."

"You bet we're the Fernald family—every man-Jack of us—not one missing."

"Oh, Marietta, you dear old thing!"

"Hurry up—this is their side of the house."

"Sh-h-h—"

"Carol, your *sh-h-ishes* would wake the dead!"

Stumbling over their own feet and bundles in the endeavor to be preternaturally quiet, the crew poured into the warm kitchen. Bearded Oliver, oldest of the clan; stout Edson, big Ralph, tall and slender Guy; and the two daughters of the house, Carolyn, growing plump and rosy at thirty; Nan, slim and girlish at twenty-four—they were all there. Marietta heaved a sigh of content as she looked them over.

"Well, I didn't really think you'd get here—all of you. Thank the Lord, you have. I s'pose you're tearin' hungry, bein' past 'leven. If you think you can eat quiet as cats, I'll feed you, but if you're goin' to make as much rumpus as you did comin' round the corner o' the wood shed I'll have to pack you straight off to bed up the back stairs."

They pleaded for mercy and hot food. They got it—everything that could be had that would diffuse no odor of cookery through the house. Smoking clam broth, a great pot of baked beans, cold meats, and jellies—they had no reason to complain of their reception. They ate hungrily with the appetites of winter travel.

"Say, but this is great," exulted Ralph, the stalwart, consuming a huge wedge of mince pie with a fine disregard for any consequences that might overtake him. "This alone is worth it. I haven't eaten such pie in a century. What a jolly place this old kitchen is! Let's have a candy pull to-morrow. I haven't been home Christmas in—let me see—I believe it's six . . . seven—yes, seven years. Look here: There's been some excuse for me, but what about you people that live near?"

He looked accusingly about. Carolyn got up and came around to him. "Don't talk about it tonight," she whispered. "We haven't any of us realized how long it's been."

"We'll get off to bed now," Guy declared, rising. "I can't get over the feeling that they may catch us down here. If either of them should want some hot water or any-thing—"

"The dining room door's bolted," Marietta assured him, "but it might need explainin' if I had to bring 'em hot water by way of the parlor. Now, go awful careful up them stairs. They're pretty near over your ma's head, but I don't dare have you tramp through the sittin' room to the front ones. Now, remember that seventh stair creaks like Ned— you've got to step right on the outside edge of it to keep it quiet. I don't know but what you boys better step right up over that seventh stair without touchin' foot to it."

"All right, we'll step!"

"Who's going to fix the bundles?" Carolyn paused to ask as she started up the stairs.

"Marietta," Guy answered. "I've labeled every one, so it'll be easy. If they hear paper rattle, they'll think it's the usual presents we've sent on, and if they come out they'll see Marietta, so it's all right. Quiet, now. Remember the seventh stair!"

They crept up, one by one, each to his or her old room. There needed to be no "doubling up," for the house was large, and each room had been left precisely as its owner had left it. It was rather ghostly, this stealing silently about with candles, and in the necessity for the suppression of speech the animation of the party rather suffered eclipse. It was late, and they were beginning to be sleepy, so they were soon in bed. But, somehow, once

167

composed for slumber, more than one grew wakeful again.

Guy, lying staring at a patch of wintry moonlight on the odd striped paper of his wall—it had stopped snowing since they had come into the house, and the clouds had broken away, leaving a brilliant sky—discovered his door to be softly opening. The glimmer of a candle filtered through the crack, a voice whispered his name.

"Who is it?" he answered under his breath.

"It's Nan. May I come in?"

"Of course. What's up?"

"Nothing. I wanted to talk a minute." She came noiselessly in, wrapped in a woolly scarlet kimono, scarlet slippers on her feet, her brown braids hanging down her back. The frost bloom lately on her cheeks had melted into a ruddy glow, her eyes were stars. She set her candle on the little stand, and she sat on the edge of Guy's bed. He raised himself on his elbow and lay looking appreciatively at her.

"This is like old times," he said. "But won't you be cold?"

"Not a bit. I'm only going to stay a minute. Anyhow, this thing is warm as toast. . . . Yes, isn't it like old times?"

"Got your lessons for tomorrow?"

She laughed. "All but my Caesar. You'll help me with that in the morning, won't you?"

"Sure, if you'll make some cushions for my bobs."

"I will. Guy—how's Lucy Harper?"

"She's all right. How's Bob Fields?"

"Oh, I don't care for him, now!" She tossed her head.

He kept up the play. "Like Dave Strong better, huh? He's a softy."

"He isn't. Oh, Guy, I heard you had a new girl."

"New girl nothing. Don't care for girls."

"Yes, you do. At least I think you do. Her name's . . . Margaret."

The play ceased abruptly. Guy's face changed. "Perhaps I do," he murmured while his sister watched him in the candlelight.

"She won't answer yet?" she asked very gently.

"Not a word."

"You've cared a good while, haven't you, dear?"

"Seems like ages. Suppose it isn't."

"No, only two years, really caring hard. Plenty of time left."

He moved his head impatiently. "Yes, if I didn't mind seeing her smile on Tommy Gower—de'il take him—just as sweetly as she smiles on me. If she ever held out the tip of her finger to me, I'd seize it and hold onto it for fair. But she doesn't. She won't. And she's going South next week for the rest of the winter, and there's a fellow down there

169

in South Carolina where she goes. Oh, he—he's redheaded after her, like the rest of us. And, well, I'm up against it good and hard, Nan, and that's the truth."

"Poor boy. And you gave up going to see her on Christmas Day, and came down here into the country just to—"

"Just to get even with myself for the way I've neglected 'em these two years while my head's been so full of *her*. It isn't fair. After last year I'd have come home today if it had meant I had to lose—well, Margaret knows I'm here. I don't know what she thinks."

"I don't believe, Guy, boy, she thinks the less of you. Yes. I must go. It will all come right in the end, dear. I'm sure of it. No, I don't know how Margaret feels. Good night, good night!"

Christmas morning, breaking upon a wintry world, the Star in the East long set. Outside the house a great silence of drift-wrapped hill and plain; inside, a crackling fire upon a wide hearth, and a pair of elderly people waking to a lonely holiday.

Mrs. Fernald crept to the door of her room—the injured knee always made walking difficult after a night's quiet. She meant to sit down by the fire which she had lately heard Marietta stirring and feeding into activity, and warm herself at its flame. She remembered with a sad little smile that she and John had hung their stockings there, and looked to see what miracle had been wrought in the night.

"Father!" Her voice caught in her throat. What was all this? By some mysterious influence her husband learned that she was calling him, though he had not really heard. He came to the door and looked at her, then at the chimneypiece where the stockings hung—a long row of them, as they had not hung since the children grew up. Stockings of quality: one of brown silk, Nan's; a fine gray sock with scarlet clocks, Ralph's; all stuffed to the top, with bundles overflowing upon the chimneypiece and even to the floor below.

"What's this? What's this?" John Fernald's voice was puzzled. "Whose are these?" He limped closer. He put on his spectacles and stared hard at a parcel protruding from the sock with the scarlet clocks.

"'Merry Christmas to Ralph from Nan,'" he read. "'To Ralph from Nan,'" he repeated vaguely. His gaze turned to his wife. His eyes were wide like a child's. But she was getting to her feet, from the chair into which she had dropped.

"The children!" she was saying. "They—they—John! They must be *here!*"

He followed her through the chilly hall to the front staircase, seldom used now, and up—as rapidly as those slow, stiff joints would allow. Trembling, Mrs. Fernald pushed open the first door at the top.

A rumpled brown head raised itself from among the pillows, a pair of sleepy but affectionate brown eyes smiled back at the two faces peering in, and a voice brimful of mirth cried softly: "Merry Christmas Mammy and Daddy!" They stared at her, their eyes growing misty. *It was their little daughter Nan, not yet grown up!*

They could not believe it. Even when they had been to every room: had seen their big son Ralph, still sleeping, his yet youthful face, full of healthy color, pillowed on his brawny arm, and his mother had gently kissed him awake to be half strangled in his hug; when they had met Edson's hearty laugh as he fired a pillow at them, carefully, so that his father could catch it; when they had seen plump pretty Carol pulling on her stockings as she sat on the floor smiling up at them; Oliver, advancing to meet them in his bathrobe and slippers; Guy, holding out both arms from above his blankets, and shouting "Merry Christmas!—and how do you like your children?" Even then it was difficult to realize that not one was missing and that no one else was there. Unconsciously Mrs. Fernald found herself looking about for the sons' wives and daughters' husbands and children. She loved them all; yet, to have her own, and no others, just for this one day—it was happiness indeed.

When they were all downstairs, about the fire, there was great rejoicing. They had Marietta in; indeed, she had been hovering continuously in the background, to the apparently frightful jeopardy of the breakfast in preparation, upon which, nevertheless, she had managed to keep a practiced eye.

"And you were in it, Marietta?" Mr. Fernald said to her in astonishment, when he first saw her. "How in the world did you get all these people into the house and to bed without waking us?"

"It was pretty consid'able of a risk," Marietta replied, with modest pride, "seein' as how they was inclined to be middlin' lively. But I kep' a-hushin' 'em up, and I filled 'em up so full of victuals they couldn't talk. I didn't know's there'd be any eatables left for today," she added, which last remark, since she had been slyly baking for a week, Guy thought might be considered pure bluff.

At the breakfast table, while the eight heads were bent, this thanksgiving arose, as the master of the house, in a voice not quite steady, offered it to One Unseen:

> *Thou who camest to us on that first Christmas Day, we*
> *bless Thee for this good and perfect gift Thou sendest us*
> *today, that Thou forgettest us not in these later years,*
> *but givest us the greatest joy of our lives in these our*
> *loyal children.*

Nan's hand clutched Guy's under the table. "Doesn't that make it worth it?" his grasp said to her, and hers replied with a frantic pressure, "Indeed it does, but we don't deserve it."

It was late in the afternoon, a tremendous Christmas dinner well over, and the group scattered, when Guy and his mother sat alone by the fire. The "boys" had gone out to the great stock barn with their father to talk over with him every detail of the prosperous business he, with the help of an invaluable assistant, was yet able to manage. Carolyn and Nan had ostensibly gone with them, but in reality the former was calling upon an old friend of her childhood, and the latter had begged a horse and sleigh and driven merrily away alone upon an errand she would tell no one but her mother.

Mrs. Fernald sat in her low chair at the side of the hearth, her son upon a cushion at her feet, his head resting against her knee. Her slender fingers were gently threading the thick locks of his hair, as she listened while he talked to her of everything in his life, and, at last, of the one thing he cared most about.

"Sometimes I get desperate and think I may as well give her up for good and all," he was saying. "She's so—so—*elusive*. I don't know any other word for it. I never can tell how I stand with her. She's going South next week. I've asked her to answer me before she goes. Somehow I've clung to the hope that I'd get my answer today. You'll laugh, but I left word with my office boy to wire me if a note or anything from her came. It's four o'clock, and I haven't heard. She—you see, I can't help thinking it's because she's going to . . . turn me down . . . and . . . hates to do it Christmas Day!"

He turned suddenly and buried his face in his mother's lap; his shoulders heaved a little in spite of himself. His mother's hand caressed his head more tenderly than ever, but, if he could have seen, her eyes were very bright.

They were silent for a long time. Then suddenly a jingle of sleigh bells approached through the falling winter twilight, drew near, and stopped at the door. Guy's mother laid her hands upon his shoulders. "Son," she said, "there's someone stopping now. Perhaps it's the boy with a message from the station."

He was on his feet in an instant. Her eyes followed him as he rushed away through the hall. Then she rose and quietly closed the sitting room door behind him.

As Guy flung open the front door, a tall and slender figure in gray furs and a wide gray hat was coming up the walk. Eyes whose glance had long been his dearest torture met Guy Fernald's and fell. Lips like which there were no others in the world smiled tremulously in response to his eager exclamation. And over the piquant young face rose an exquisite color which was not altogether born of the wintry air. The girl who for two years had been only "elusive" had taken the significant step of coming to North Estabrook in response to an eloquent telephone message sent that morning by Nan.

Holding both her hands fast, Guy led her up into the house, and found himself alone with her in the shadowy hall. With one gay shout Nan had driven away toward the barn. The inner doors were all closed. Blessing the wondrous sagacity of his womankind, Guy took advantage of his moment.

"Nan brought you, I see that. I know you're very fond of her, but—you didn't come wholly to please her, did you, Margaret?"

"Not wholly."

"I've been looking all day for my answer. I—oh, I wonder if"—he was gathering courage from her aspect, which for the first time in his experience failed to keep him at a distance—"*dare* I think you *bring it?*"

She slowly lifted her face. "I thought it was so—so dear of you," she murmured, "to come home to your people instead of . . . staying with me. I thought you deserved . . . what you say . . . you want—"

"Margaret, you—"

"I haven't given you any Christmas present. Will . . . *I* . . . do?"

"Will *you* do! *Oh!*" It was a great explosive sigh of relief and joy, and as he gave vent to it he caught her close. "Will . . . *you* . . . do? . . . *Will you do!* . . . I rather *think you will!*"

"Emeline—"

"Yes, John dear?"

"You're not . . . crying?"

"Oh, no! No, no, John!" What a blessing deafness is sometimes! The ear cannot detect the delicate tremolo which might tell the story too plainly. And in the darkness of night, the eye cannot see.

"It's been a pretty nice day, hasn't it?"

"A beautiful day!"

177

"I guess there's no doubt but the children care a good deal for the old folks yet."

"No doubt at all, dear."

"It's good to think they're all asleep under the roof once more, isn't it? And one extra one. We like her, don't we?"

"Oh, very, very much!"

"Yes, Guy's done well. I always thought he'd get her, if he hung on. The Fernalds always hang on, but Guy's got a mite of a temper. I didn't know but he might let go a little too soon. Well, it's great to think they all plan to spend every Christmas Day with us, isn't it, Emeline?"

"Yes, dear. It's great."

"Well, I must let you go to sleep. It's been a big day, and I guess you're tired. Emeline, we've not only got each other. We've got the children, too. That's a pretty happy thing at our age, isn't it, now?"

"Yes. Yes."

"Good night—Christmas Night, Emeline."

"Good night, dear."

Christmas, Lost and Found

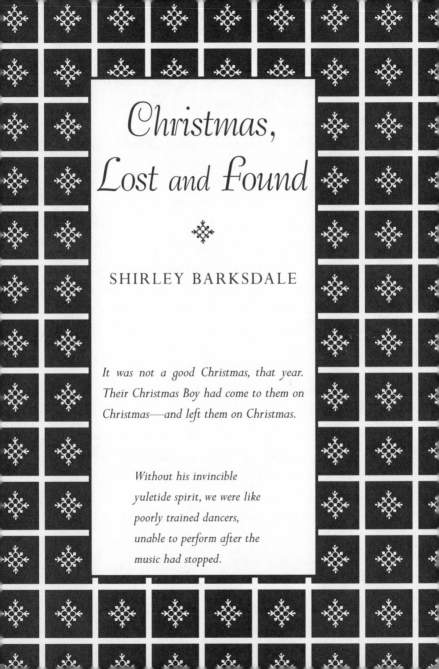

❖

SHIRLEY BARKSDALE

It was not a good Christmas, that year. Their Christmas Boy had come to them on Christmas—and left them on Christmas.

Without his invincible yuletide spirit, we were like poorly trained dancers, unable to perform after the music had stopped.

But now, sixteen years after they had fled all their son had known and loved, they had returned. Why, they really didn't know. But here they were.

And then they heard the screech of car brakes . . .

This little story, born in a 1988 McCall's, *and quickly picked up by* Reader's Digest, *has become, for many, a cherished Christmas tradition. Shirley Barksdale still lives and writes from Denver.*

We called him our Christmas Boy because he came to us during that season of joy, when he was just six days old. Already his eyes twinkled more brightly than the lights on his first tree.

Later, as our family expanded, he made it clear that only he had the expertise to select and decorate the tree each year. He rushed the season, starting his gift list before we'd even finished the Thanksgiving turkey. He pressed us into singing carols, our croaky voices sounding more frog-like than ever compared to his perfect pitch. He stirred us up, led us through a round of merry chaos.

Then, on his twenty-fourth Christmas, he left us as unexpectedly as he had come. A car accident, on an icy Denver street, on his way home to his young wife and infant daughter. But first he had stopped by the family home to decorate our tree, a ritual he had never abandoned.

Without his invincible yuletide spirit, we were like poorly trained dancers, unable to perform after the music had stopped. In our grief, his father and I sold our home, where memories clung to every room. We moved to California, leaving behind our support system of friends and church. All the wrong moves.

It seemed I had come full circle, back to those early years when there had been just my parents and me. Christmas had always been a quiet, hurried affair, unlike the celebrations at my friends' homes, which were lively and peopled with rollicking relatives. I vowed then that someday I'd marry and have six children, and that at Christmas my house would vibrate with energy and love.

I found the man who shared my dream, but we had not reckoned on the surprise of infertility. Undaunted, we applied for adoption, ignoring gloomy prophecies that an adopted child would not be the same as "our own flesh and blood." Even then, hope did not run high; the waiting list was long. But against all odds, within a year he arrived and was ours. Then Nature surprised us again, and in rapid succession we added two biological children to the family. Not as many as we had hoped for, but compared to my quiet childhood, three made an entirely satisfactory crowd.

Those friends were right about adopted children not being the same. He wasn't the least like the rest of us. Through his own unique heredity, he brought color into our lives with his gift of music, his irrepressible good cheer, his bossy wit. He made us look and behave better than we were.

In the sixteen years that followed his death, time added chapters to our lives. His widow remarried and had a son; his daughter graduated from high school. His brother married and began his own Christmas traditions in another state. His sister, an artist, seemed fulfilled by her career. His father and I grew old enough to retire, and in December of 1987 we decided to return to Denver. The call home was unclear; we knew only that we yearned for some indefinable connection, for something lost that had to be retrieved before time ran out.

We slid into Denver on the tail end of a blizzard. Blocked highways forced us through the city, past the Civic Center, ablaze with thousands of lights—a scene I was not ready to face. This same trek had been one of our Christmas Boy's favorite holiday traditions. He had been relentless in his insistence that we all pile into the car, its windows fogged over with our warm breath, its tires fighting for a grip in ice.

I looked away from the lights and fixed my gaze on the distant Rockies, where he had loved to go barreling up the mountainside in search of the perfect tree. Now in the foothills there was his grave—a grave I could not bear to visit.

Once we were settled in the small, boxy house, so different from the family home where we had orchestrated our lives, we hunkered down like two barn swallows who had missed the last migration South. While I stood staring toward the snowcapped mountains one day, I heard the sudden screech of car brakes, then the impatient peal of the doorbell. There stood our granddaughter, and in the gray-green eyes and impudent grin I saw the reflection of our Christmas Boy.

Behind her, lugging a large pine tree, came her mother, stepfather, and nine-year-old half brother. They swept past us in a flurry of laughter; they uncorked the sparkling cider and toasted our homecoming. Then they decorated the tree and piled gaily wrapped packages under the boughs.

❖

"You'll recognize the ornaments," said my former daughter-in-law. "They were his. I saved them for you."

"I picked out most of the gifts, Grandma," said the nine-year-old, whom I hardly knew.

When I murmured, in remembered pain, that we hadn't had a tree for, well, sixteen years, our cheeky granddaughter said, "Then it's time to shape up!"

They left in a whirl, shoving one another out the door, but not before asking us to join them the next morning for church, then dinner at their home.

"Oh, we just can't," I began.

"You sure can," ordered our granddaughter, as bossy as her father had been. "I'm singing the solo, and I want to see you there."

"Bring earplugs," advised the nine-year-old.

We had long ago given up the poignant Christmas services, but now, under pressure, we sat rigid in the front pew, fighting back tears.

Then it was solo time. Our granddaughter swished (her father would have swaggered) to center stage, and the magnificent voice soared, clear and true, in perfect pitch. She sang "O Holy Night," which brought back bittersweet memories. In a rare emotional response, the congregation applauded in delight. How her father would have relished that moment.

We had been alerted that there would be a "whole mess of people" for dinner—but thirty-five? Assorted relatives filled every corner of the house; small children, noisy and exuberant, seemed to bounce off the walls. I could not sort out who belonged to whom, but it didn't matter. They all belonged to one another. They took us in, enfolded us in joyous camaraderie. We sang carols in loud, off-key voices, saved only by that amazing soprano.

Sometime after dinner, before the winter sunset, it occurred to me that a true family is not always one's own flesh and blood. It is a climate of the heart. Had it not been for our adopted son, we would not now be surrounded by caring strangers who would help us to hear the music again.

Later, not yet ready to give up the day, our granddaughter asked us to come along with her. "I'll drive," she said. "There's a place I like to go." She jumped behind the wheel of the car and, with the confidence of a newly licensed driver, zoomed off toward the foothills.

Alongside the headstone rested a small, heart-shaped rock, slightly cracked, painted by our artist daughter. On its weathered surface she had written: TO MY BROTHER, WITH LOVE. Across the crest of the grave lay a holly-bright Christmas wreath. Our number-two son admitted, when asked, that he sent one every year.

In the chilly but somehow comforting silence, we were not prepared for our unpredictable granddaughter's next move. Once more that day her voice, so like her father's, lifted in song, and the mountainside echoed the chorus of "Joy to the World," on and on into infinity.

When the last pure note had faded, I felt, for the first time since our son's death, a sense of peace, of the positive continuity of life, of renewed faith and hope. The real meaning of Christmas had been restored to us. Hallelujah!

"Meditation"
in a Minor
Key

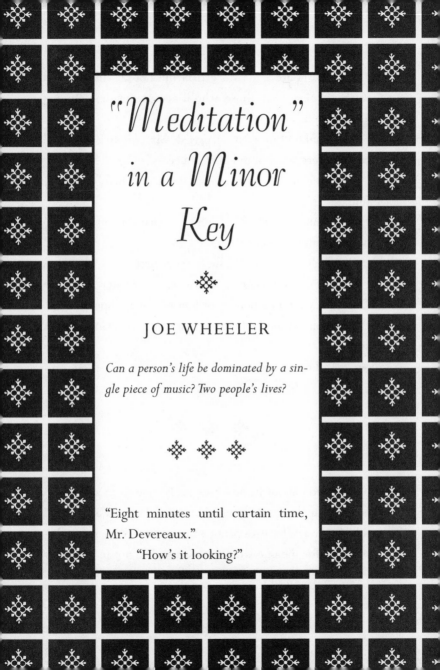

JOE WHEELER

Can a person's life be dominated by a single piece of music? Two people's lives?

"Eight minutes until curtain time, Mr. Devereaux."

"How's it looking?"

"Full house. No. More than full house—they're already turning away those who'll accept Standing Room Only tickets."

"Frankly, I'm a bit surprised, Mr. Schobel. My last concert here was not much of a success."

"I remember, sir. . . . The house was barely a third full."

"Hmm. I wonder . . . uh . . . what do you suppose has made the difference?"

"Well, for one thing, sir, it's your first-ever Christmas concert. For another, people are regaining interest—that Deutsche Grammophon recording has all Europe talking. But pardon me, sir. I'd better let you get ready. Good luck, sir."

And he was gone.

No question about it, he mused as he bowed to acknowledge the applause, the venerable Opera House was indeed full. As always, his eyes panned the sea of faces as he vainly searched for the one who never came, had not in ten long years. He had *so* hoped tonight would be different. That package—it hadn't done the job after all. . . .

Ten years ago tonight it was. Right here in Old Vienna. It was to have been the happiest Christmas Eve in his life: Was Ginevra not to become his bride the next day?

What a fairy-tale courtship that had been. It had all started at the Salzburg Music Festival, where he was the center of attention—not only of the city, but of the world. Had he not stunned concertgoers by his incredible coup? The first pianist to ever win grand piano's Triple Crown: the Van Cliburn, the Queen Elizabeth, and the Tchaikovsky competitions?

Fame had built steadily for him as one after another of the great prizes had fallen to him. Now, as reporters, interviewers, and cameramen followed his every move, he grew drunk on the wine of adulation.

It happened as he leaned over the parapet of Salzburg Castle, watching the morning sun gild the rooftops of the city below. He had risen early in order to hike up the hill to the castle and watch the sunrise. A cool alpine breeze ruffled the trees just above; but it also displaced a few strands of raven black hair only a few feet to his left. Their glances met, and they both glanced away, only to blush as they glanced back. She was the most beautiful girl he had ever seen. But beautiful in more than mere appearance: beautiful in poise and grace as well. Later, he would gradually discover her beauty of soul.

With uncharacteristic shyness, he introduced himself to her. And then she withdrew in confusion as she tied the name to the cover stories. Disarming her with a smile, he quickly changed the subject: What was *she* doing in Salzburg?

As it turned out, she was in Europe for a summerlong study tour—and how his heart leaped when she admitted that her study group was staying in Salzburg the entire week. He made the most of it: Before her bus had moved on he had pried from her not very reluctant fingers a copy of the tour itinerary.

And like Jean Valjean's inexorable nemesis, Javert, he pursued her all over Europe, driving his concert manager into towering rages. Had he forgotten that there was the long and arduous fall schedule to prepare for? Had he forgotten the time it took to memorize a new repertoire? No, he hadn't forgotten: the truth of the matter was that his priorities had suddenly changed. Every midweek, in around-the-clock marathons, he'd give his practicing its due—then he'd escape in order to be with Ginevra for the weekend.

They were instant soul mates: They both loved the

mountains and the sea, dawn and dusk, Tolstoy and Twain, snow and sand, hiking and skiing, gothic cathedrals and medieval castles, sidewalk cafes and old bookstores. But they were not clones: In art, she loved Georges de la Tour and Caravaggio whereas his patron saints were Dürer and Hieronymus Bosch; in music, he preferred Mozart and Prokofiev whereas she reveled in Chopin and Liszt.

He knew the day he met her that, for him, there would never be another woman. He was that rarity: a man who out of the whole world will choose but one—and if that one be denied him . . .

But he wasn't denied. It was on the last day of her stay, just hours before she boarded her plane for home, that he asked her to climb with him the zigzagging inner staircases of the bell tower of Votivkirche, that great neo-Gothic cathedral of Vienna, paling in comparison only with its legendary ancestor, St. Stephens.

Far up in the tower, breathing hard for more than one reason, his voice shook as he took both her hands captive and looked through her honest eyes into her heart—his, he knew, even without asking. She never *did* actually say yes, for the adorable curl of her lips, coupled with the candlelit road to heaven in her eyes, was her undoing.

The rapture which followed comes only once in a lifetime, when it comes at all.

Then the scene changed, and he stiffened as if receiving a mortal blow, for but four months later, in that self-same bell tower, his world had come to an end. That terrible, terrible night when his nuptial dreams were slain by a violin.

Ginevra drew her heavy coat tighter around her as the airport limousine disappeared into the night. Inside the Opera House she made her way to the ticket counter to ask for directions to her section.

From the other side of the doors she heard Bach's "Italian Concerto" being reborn. She listened intently. She had not been mistaken after all: A change *had* taken place.

Leaning against a pillar, she let the distant notes wash over her while she took the scroll of her life and unrolled a third of it. How vividly she remembered that memorable fall. Michael's letters came as regularly as night following day: long letters most of the time, short messages when his hectic schedule precluded more. Her pattern was unvarying: She would walk up the mountain road to the mailbox, out of the day's mail search for that precious envelope, then carry it unopened on top of the rest of the mail back to the chalet, perched high on a promontory point 1,600 feet above the Denver plain. Then she'd walk out onto the upper deck and seat herself. Off to her right were the Flatirons massed above the city of Boulder, front center below was the skyline of Denver—at night a fairyland of twinkling lights—and to the left the mountains stair-stepped up to 14,255 foot Longs Peak and Rocky Mountain National Park. Then she'd listen for the pines—oh! those heavenly pines! They would be soughing their haunting song . . . and *then* she would open his letter.

So full of romance were her starlit eyes that weeks passed before she realized there was a hairline crack in her heart—and Michael was the cause of it. She hadn't realized it during that idyllic summer as the two of them had spent so much time exploring Gothic cathedrals, gazing transfixed as light transformed stained-glass into heart-stopping glory, sitting on transepts as organists opened their stops and called on their pipes to dare the red zone of reverberating sound.

She finally, in a long letter, asked him point-blank whether or not he believed in God. His response was a masterpiece of subterfuge and fence-straddling for well he knew how central the Lord was to her. As women have ever since the dawn of time, she rationalized that if he just loved *her* enough—and surely he *did*—then of course he would come to love God as much as she.

So it was that she put her reservations and premonitions aside, and deflected her parents' concerns in that respect as well. Michael had decided he wanted to be married in the same cathedral where he had proposed to her, and as it was large enough to accommodate family as well as key figures of the music world, she had reluctantly acquiesced. Personally, she would have much rather been married in the small Boulder church high up on Mapleton Avenue. A Christmas wedding there, in the church she so loved . . . but it was not to be.

Deciding to make the best of it, she and her family drove down the mountain, took the freeway to Stapleton Airport, boarded the plane, and found their seats. As the big United jet roared off the runway, she looked out the window at Denver and her beloved Colorado receding below her. She wondered: Could Michael's European world ever really take its place?

It was cold that memorable Christmas Eve, and the snow lay several feet deep on Viennese streets. Ginevra, ever the romantic, shyly asked Michael if he would make a special pilgrimage with her.

"Where to?" queried Michael, "It's mighty cold outside."

"The bell tower of Votivkirche."

He grinned that boyish grin she loved. "I really *am* marrying a sentimentalist, aren't I? Oh well," he complained good-naturedly, "I guess I'd better get used to it. Let's find our coats."

An unearthly quiet came over the great city as they once again climbed the winding staircases of Votivkirche. She caught her breath at the beauty of it all when they at last reached their eyrie and looked down at the frosted rooftops and streets below. Michael, however, much preferred the vision *she* represented, in her flame-colored dress and sable coat.

Then it was, faintly and far away, that they heard it. They never did trace its origin exactly. It might have wafted its way up the tower from below or it might have come from an apartment across the way. Ordinarily, in the cacophony of the city, they could not possibly have heard it, but tonight, with snow deadening the street sounds, they could distinctly pick up every note. Whoever the violinist was, was a master.

Ginevra listened, transfixed. Michael, noting her tear-stained cheeks, shattered the moment with an ill-timed laugh. "Why you old crybaby, it's nothing but a song! I've heard it somewhere before. . . . I don't remember who wrote it, but it's certainly nothing to cry over."

He checked as he saw her recoil as if he had slashed

199

her face with a whip. Her face blanched, and she struggled for control. After a long pause, she said in a toneless voice: "It is not a song. It is 'Meditation' by Massenet."

"Well, that's fine with me," quipped Michael. "I'll just meditate about *you.*"

There was a long silence, and now, quite ill at ease, he shuffled his feet and tried to pass it all off as a joke.

But in that, he failed abysmally: "You . . . you don't hear it at all," she cried. "You just don't. . . . I never hear that melody without tears, or without soaring to Heaven on the notes. Massenet *had* to have been a Christian! And, furthermore, whoever plays it like we just heard it played *has* to be a Christian, too!"

"Oh, come now, Ginevra. Aren't you getting carried away by a simple little ditty? *Anyone* who really knows how to play the violin could play it just as well. *I* certainly could—and I don't even believe in . . . in God—" He stopped, vainly trying to slam his lips on the words in time, but perversely they slipped out of their own accord.

Deep within the citadel of her innermost being, Ginevra felt her heart shudder as if seized by two powerful opposing forces then: Where the hairline crack of her heart once was there was an awful *crack,* and a yawning fault took its place.

The look of agony on her face brought him to his senses at last, but it was too late. She looked at him with glaciered cheeks and with eyes so frozen that he could barely discern the tiny flickering that had, only moments ago, almost overpowered him with the glow of a thousand love-lit candles.

She turned, slipped something which had once been on her finger into his coat pocket, and was gone. So quickly was the act done that at first he failed to realize she was no longer there. Then he called after her and ran blindly down the stairs. Ginevra, however, with the instinct of a wounded animal, found an unlocked stairwell door and hid inside until he had raced down the tower and into the street. Much later, she silently made her way out into a world made glad by midnight bells. But there was no Christmas gladness in *her* heart.

She determined to never see him again. Neither his calls nor his letters nor his telegrams would she answer. She wrote him only once: "Please do not *ever* try to contact me in any way again."

And he—his pride in shreds—never had.

Never would he forget that awful Christmas when—*alone*—he had to face the several thousand wedding guests and the importunate press with the news that it was all off. No, he could give them no reasons. And then he had fled.

Since he had planned on an extended honeymoon he had no more concerts scheduled until the next fall. That winter and spring he spent much time in solitude, moping and feeling sorry for himself. By late spring, he was stir-crazy, so he fled to the South Pacific, to Asia, to Africa, to South America—*anywhere* to get away from himself and his memories.

Somehow, by midsummer, he began to regain control; he returned to Europe and quickly mastered his fall repertoire. That fall, most of his reviews were of the rave variety, for he dazzled with his virtuosity and technique.

For several years, his successes continued, and audiences filled concert halls wherever he performed. But there came a day when that was no longer true, when he realized that most dreaded of performing world truths: that it was all over; he had peaked. Here he was, his career hardly begun, and his star was already setting. But *why?*

Reviewers and concertgoers alike tried vainly to diagnose the ailment and prescribe medicinal cures, but nothing worked. More and more the tenor of the reviews began to sound like the following:

How sad it is that Devereaux—once thought to be the
rising star of our age, the worthy successor to
Horowitz—has been revealed as but human clay after
all. It is as if he represents but a case of arrested
development. Normally, as a pianist lives and ages, the
roots sink deeper and the storm-battered trunk and
branches develop seasoning and rugged strength. Not
so with Devereaux. It's as if all growth ceased some
time ago. Oh! No one can match him when it comes to
razzle-dazzle and special effects, but one gets a bit
tired of these when there is no offsetting depth.

Like a baseball slugger in a prolonged batting slump, Michael tried everything: He dabbled in every philosophy or mysticism he came across. Like a drunken bee, he reeled from flower to flower without any real sense of direction.

And "Meditation" had gradually become an obsession with him: He just couldn't seem to get it out of his consciousness. He determined to prove to her that you didn't have to be religious in order to play it well. But as much as he tried, as much as he applied his vaunted techniques and interpretive virtuosity to it, it remained as flat, stale, and unmoving as three-hour-old coffee.

He even went to the trouble of researching the tune's

203

origins, feeling confident that it, like much music concert performers play, would apparently have no religious connections whatsoever. In his research, he discovered that "Meditation" came from Massenet's opera *Thaïs,* which he knew had to do with a dissolute courtesan. Aha! He had her! But then, he dug deeper and discovered, to his chagrin, that although it was true that Thaïs had a dissolute sexual past, as was true with Mary Magdalene, she was redeemed, and "Meditation" represents the intermezzo bridge between the pagan past of the first two acts and the oneness with God in the third act.

So he had to acknowledge defeat here, too.

As for Ginevra, she was never far from his thoughts. But not once would his pride permit him to ask anyone about her, her career, or whether or not she had ever married.

He just *existed* . . . and measured his life by concerts and hotel rooms.

Ginevra, too, after the long numbness and shock had at last weathered into a reluctant peace, belatedly realized that life had to go on, but just what should she do with her life?

It was during a freak spring blizzard which snowed her in that the answer came. She had been sitting in the conversation pit of the three-story-high massive moss rock fireplace, gazing dreamily into the fire, when suddenly, the mood came upon her to write. She reached for a piece of paper, picked up her Pilot pen, and began writing a poem. A poem about pain, disillusion, and heartbreak. The next day, she mailed it off to a magazine. Not long after, it was published.

She decided to do graduate work in the humanities and in education. She completed, along the way, a master's, and later a Ph.D.; in the process, becoming the world's foremost authority on the life and times of a woman writer of the American heartland. She also continued, as her busy schedule permitted, to write poems, essays, short stories, inspirational literature, and longer works of fiction.

So it was that Ginevra became a teacher: a teacher of writing, of literature—and life. Each class was a microcosm of life itself; in each class were souls crying out to be ministered to, to be appreciated, to be loved.

Because of her charm, vivacity, joie de vivre, and sense of humor, she became ever more popular and beloved with the passing of the years. She attracted suitors like children to a toy store. Yet, though some of these friendships got to the threshold of love, none of them got any farther:

It was as if not one of them could match what she had left behind in Vienna.

The good Lord it was who saw her through, who shored up her frailties and helped to mend the brokenness.

Meanwhile, she did find time to keep up with Michael's life and career. In doing so, she bought all his recordings, playing them often. Yet, she was vaguely dissatisfied: She, too, noted the lack of growth—and wondered.

One balmy day in late November during the seventh year after the breakup, as she was walking down the ridge to her home, she stopped to listen to her two favorite sounds: the cascading creek cavorting its way down to the Front Range plain and the sibilant whispering of the pines. Leaning against a large rock, she looked up at that incredibly blue sky of the Colorado high country.

As always, her thoughts refused to stay in their neat little cages. She had tried all kinds of locks during those seven years, but not one of them worked. And now, when she had thought them safely locked in, here came all her truant thoughts: bounding up to her like a ragtag litter of exuberant puppies, overjoyed at finding her hiding place.

And every last one of the little mutts was yelping Michael's name.

What would *he* be doing this Christmas? It bothered

her—had bothered her for almost seven years now—that her own judge had refused to acquit her for her Michael-related words and actions. Periodically, during these years, she had submitted her case to the judge in the courthouse of her mind; and every last time, after listening to the evidence, the judge had looked at her stern-faced. She would bang the gavel on the judicial bench and intone severely: "Insufficient evidence on which to absolve you. Next case?"

She couldn't get out of her head an article she had read several months before—an article about Michael Devereaux. The writer, who had interviewed her subject in depth, had done her homework well: for the portrait of Michael rang true to Ginevra. The individual revealed in the character sketch was both the Michael Ginevra knew and a Michael she would rather not know. The interviewer pointed out that Michael was a rather bitter man for one so young in years. So skittish had the interviewee been whenever approached on the subject of women in his life, that the writer postulated that it was her personal conviction that somewhere along the way Devereaux had been terribly hurt by someone he loved deeply. Here, Ginevra winced. The writer concluded her character portrait with a disturbing synthesis: "Devereaux, his concert career floundering, appears to be searching for answers. But he's not looking in the direction of God. Like many, if not most, Europeans of our time, he appears to be almost totally secular; thus he has nowhere but within himself upon which to draw strength and inspiration. Sadly, his inner wells appear to retain only shallow reservoirs from which to draw. . . . A pity."

A nagging thought returned to tug at her heartstrings: What had *she* done—what had she *ever* done—to show Michael a better way? "But," she retorted, "I don't want him to become a Christian just for *me!*" But this time that oft-used cop-out didn't suffice. She kept seeing that stern-faced judge within. . . . In the long, long silence which followed was born a plan of action. If it worked, if he responded as she hoped he might, sooner or later, she would *know!* For inescapably, the secret would "out" through his music.

She determined to implement her plan of action that very day.

Several weeks after Ginevra's decision, Michael had returned to his hotel after a concert, a particularly unsatisfactory one—and it seemed these days that there were more and more of this kind. Even the crowd had been smaller than any he could remember in years. He was convinced that his career and life were both failures—and that there was little reason to remain living. He went to bed and vainly tried to sleep. After an hour or two of thrashing around, he got up, turned on the light, and looked for the last packet of mail forwarded to him by his agent. There was something in it that intrigued him. Ah! Here it was.

A small registered package had arrived from New York. There was no return address, and he didn't recognize the handwriting on the mailer. Inside was a slim, evidently long-out-of-print book titled *The Other Wise Man* written by an author he had never heard of: Henry Van Dyke. Well, it looked like a quick read and he couldn't sleep anyhow. . . .

A quick read it was not: He found himself rereading certain passages several times. It was after 3 A.M. before he finally put it down. He was moved in spite of himself. Then, he retired, this time to sleep.

During that Christmas season, he reread it twice more—and each time he read it he wondered what had motivated that unknown person to send it.

Three months later came another registered packet from New York. It too was obviously a book and, to his joy, another old one. To his relief—for he had an intense fear of

God and religion—it did not appear to be a religious book. The author and title were alike unknown to him: Myrtle Reed's *The Master's Violin*. The exquisite metallic lamination of this turn-of-the-century first edition quite took his breath away. *Someone* had spent some money on *this* gift! He read it that night, and it seemed, in some respects, that the joy and pain he vicariously experienced in the reading mirrored his own. And the violin! It brought back memories of that melody, that melody which just would not let him go, that melody which represented the high tide of his life.

It was mid-June, three months later, when the next registered package arrived from New York. This time, his hands were actually trembling as he opened the package. Another book by yet another author he had never heard of: Harold Bell Wright. Kind of a strange title it had: *That Printer of Udel's*. But it was old and had a tipped-in cover: the combination was irresistible. He dropped everything and started to read.

He was not able to put it down. In it he saw depicted a portrait of Christian living unlike any he had ever seen before: a way of life which had to do not just with sterile doctrine but with a living, loving outreach to one's fellow man. He finished the book late that night. A month later, he read it again.

By late September, he had been watching his mail with great anticipation for some time; What would it be this time? Then it came: another book, first published in 1907, by the same author as the last book, with the intriguing title: *The Calling of Dan Matthews.* It made the same impact upon him which its predecessor had. Nevertheless, Michael was no easy nut to crack. He continued to keep his jury sequestered—he was nowhere near ready for a verdict of any kind.

Early in December arrived his second Van Dyke: *The Mansion,* a lovely lime-green illustrated edition. This book spawned some exceedingly disturbing questions about his inner motivations. Of what value, really, was *his* life? When was the last time he had ever done anything for someone without expecting something in return? For such a small book, it certainly stirred up some difficult-to-answer questions!

March brought a book he had often talked about reading, but never had the temerity to tackle: Victor Hugo's forbidding *Les Misérables:* almost 1,500 pages unabridged! He wondered: *Why!* Why such a literary classic following what he had been sent before? He didn't wonder long. The story of Jean Valjean was a story of redemption; the story of a man who climbed out of hell. The first

Christ figure he could ever remember seeing in French literature. By now, he was beginning to look for fictional characters who exhibited, in some manner, Christian values.

At the end of the book was a brief note:

NO OTHER BOOK FOR SIX MONTHS. REVIEW.

He did . . . but he felt terribly abused, sorely missing the expected package in June.

By the time September's leaves began to fall, he was in a state of intense longing. Certainly, after *Les Misérables*, and after a half year wait, it would have to be a blockbuster! To his amazement and disgust, it was a slim mass-market paperback with the thoroughly unappetizing title of *Mere Christianity*. The author he knew of but had never read: C. S. Lewis. Swallowing his negative feelings with great difficulty, he gingerly tested with his toes Lewis's Jordan River. As he stepped farther in, he was—quite literally—overwhelmed. Every argument he had ever thrown up as a barrier between himself and God was systematically and thoroughly demolished. He had had no idea that God and Christianity were any more than an amalgamation of feelings—for the first time, he was able to conceptualize God with his *mind!*

Whoever was sending him the books was either feeling sorry for making him wait so long or punishing him by literally burying him in print! He was kindly given two weeks to digest *Mere Christianity,* and then began the non-stop barrage of his soul. First came three shells in a row in the form of Lewis's Space Trilogy: *Out of That Silent Planet, Perelandra,* and *That Hideous Strength.* At first, Michael, like so many other readers of the books, enjoyed the plot solely on the science fiction level. Then, he wryly observed to himself that Lewis had set him up: woven into the story was God and His plan of salvation!

The Trilogy was followed by Lewis's *Screwtape Letters.* How Michael laughed as he read this one! How incredibly wily is the Great Antagonist! And how slyly Lewis had reversed the roles in order to shake up all his simplistic assumptions about the battles between Good and Evil.

A week later, another shell: *The Four Loves.* In it, Michael found himself reevaluating almost all of his people-related friendships in life. That was but the beginning: Then Lewis challenged him to explore the possibilities of a friendship with the Eternal.

Two shells then came in succession: *Surprised by Joy* and *A Grief Observed.* At long last, he was able to learn more about Lewis the man. Not only that, but how Lewis, so late in life introduced to the joys of nuptial love, related to the untimely death of his bride; how Lewis, in his wracking grief, almost lost his way—almost turned away God Him-

❖

self! Paralleling Lewis's searing loss of his beloved was Michael's loss of Ginevra: relived once again, it was bone-wrenching in its intensity. More so than Lewis's, for he had not Lewis's God to turn to in the darkest hour.

The final seven shells came in the form of what appeared to be, at first glance, a series of books for children: Lewis's Chronicles of Narnia. It took Michael some time to figure out why he had been sent this series last after such heavyweights! It was not until he was about halfway through that he knew. By then, he had fully realized just how powerful a manifestation of the attributes of Christ Aslan the lion was. By the moving conclusion of *The Last Battle,* the fifteen shells from Lewis's howitzer had made mere rubble out of what was left of Michael's defense system.

Then came a beautiful edition of the Phillips Translation of the New Testament. On the flyleaf, in neat black calligraphy, was this line:

MAY THIS BOOK HELP TO MAKE YOUR NEW YEAR TRULY NEW.

He read the New Testament with a receptive attitude, taking a month to complete it. One morning, following a concert the night before in Florence, he rose very early and walked to the Arno River to watch the sunrise. As he leaned against a lamppost, his thoughts (donning their accountant coats) did an audit of the past three years.

He was belatedly discovering that a life without God

just wasn't worth living. In fact, *nothing,* he now concluded, had any lasting meaning divorced from a higher power. He looked around him, mentally scrutinizing the lives of family members, friends, and colleagues in the music world. He noted the devastating divorce statistics, the splintered homes, and the resulting flotsam of loneliness and despair. Without God, he now concluded, no human relationship was likely to last very long.

Nevertheless, even now that he was thoroughly convinced in his mind that God represented the only way out of his dead-end existence, he bullheadedly balked at crossing the line out of the Dark into the Light.

The day before Easter of that tenth year, there came another old book, an expensive English first edition of Francis Thompson's poems. Inside, on the endsheet, was this coda to their faceless three-year friendship:

> *Dear Michael,*
> *For almost three years now,*
> *you have never been out of my*
> *thoughts and prayers.*
> *I hope that these books have come*
> *to mean to you what they do to me.*
> *This is your last book.*

❖

Please read "The Hound of Heaven."
The rest is up to you.

> *Your Friend*

Immediately, he turned to the long poem, and immersed himself in Thompson's lines. Although some of the words were a bit antiquated and jarred a little, nevertheless he felt that the lines were written laser-straight to him, especially those near the poem's gripping conclusion, for Michael identified totally with Thompson's own epic flight from the pursuing celestial Hound:

> *Whom will you find to love ignoble thee*
> *Save Me, save only Me?*
> *All which I took from thee I did but take,*
> *Not for thy harms,*
> *But just that thou might'st seek it in My arms.*
> *All which thy child's mistake*
> *Fancies as lost, I have stored for thee at home.*
> *Rise, clasp My hand, and come!*

These lines broke him . . . and he fell to his knees.

It was the morning after, and Michael awakened to the first Easter of the rest of his life. Needing very much to be alone, he decided to head for the family chalet near Mt. Blanc. How fortunate, he mused, that the rest of the family was skiing at St. Moritz that week.

Two hours before he got there, it began to snow, but his Porsche, itself born during a bitterly cold German winter, growled its delight as it devoured the road to Chamonix. It was snowing even harder when he arrived at the chalet, where Michael was greeted with delight by Jacques and Marie, the caretakers.

Breakfast was served adjacent to a roaring fire in the great alpine fireplace. Afterward, thoroughly satisfied, he leaned back in his favorite chair and looked out at the vista of falling snow.

He *felt,* he finally concluded, as if sometime in the night he had been reborn. It was as if all his life he had been carrying a staggeringly heavy backpack, a backpack into which some cruel overseer had dropped yet another five-pound brick *each* January 1 of his life, for as far back as he could remember. And now—suddenly—he was *free!* What a paradoxical revelation that was: that the long-feared surrender to God resulted in not the dreaded straitjacketed servitude, but the most incredible euphoric freedom he had ever imagined!

Looking back at the years of his life, he now recognized that he had been fighting God every step of the way, but God, refusing to give up on him, had merely kept His distance. He went to his suitcase, reached for that already precious book of poems, returned to his seat by the fire, and turned again to that riveting first stanza:

> *I fled Him, down the nights and down the days;*
> *I fled Him, down the arches of the years;*
> *I fled Him, down the labyrinthine ways*
> *Of my own mind, and in the midst of tears*
> *I hid from Him, and under running laughter.*
> *Up vistaed hopes I sped;*
> *And shot, precipitated*
> *Adown Titanic glooms of chastened fears,*
> *From those strong Feet that followed, followed after.*
> *But with unhurrying chase,*
> *And unperturbed pace,*
> *Deliberate speed, majestic instancy,*
> *They beat—and a Voice beat*

More instant than the Feet—
'All things betray thee, who betrayest Me!'

He turned away, unable, because of a blurring of his vision, to read on.

"How many *years* I have lost!" he sighed.

Years during which the frenetic pace of his life caused the Pursuing Hound to sadly drop back. Years during which he proudly strutted, wearing the tinsel crown of popularity. And then . . . that flimsy bit of ephemera was taken away and the long descent into the maelstrom had taken place. It had been in his darkest hour, when he actually felt Ultimate Night reaching for him, that he plainly and distinctly heard his Pursuer again.

For almost three years now that Pursuer had drawn ever closer. There had been a strange meshing: the Voice in the crucifixion earthquake who spoke to Artaban, the Power that defied the Ally in the Dan Matthews story, the Force revealed through the pulsating strings of "mine Cremona," the Presence which—through the Bishop's incredible act of forgiveness and compassion—saved the shackled life of Jean Valjean, the Angel who showed John Weightman's pitiful mansion to him, Malacandra of the Perelandra story and Aslan in the Narnia series. As he read "The Hound of Heaven," all the foregoing lost their distinctiveness and merged into the pursuing Hound: They were one and the same!

Michael resonated with a strange new power, a power he had never experienced before. It was as if, during the night, in his badly crippled power station (a generating facility to which, over the years, one incoming line after another had been cut, until he was reduced to but one frail piece of frayed wire that alone kept him from blackout), a new cable, with the capacity to illuminate an entire world, had been snaked down the dusty stairs, and then *plugged in.*

Then, from far back (even before his descent into hell), two images emerged out of the mists of time, one visual and one aural: the tear-stained face of the Only Woman and the throbbing notes of "Meditation."

Tingling all over, he stood up and walked over to the grand piano always kept in the lodge for his practicing needs, lifted up the lid, seated himself on the bench, and looked up. Humbly, he asked the question: "Am I ready at last, Lord?"

Then he reached for the keys and began to play. As his fingers swept back and forth, something else occurred: For the first time in over nine years, he was able—without printed music—to replay in his mind every note, every intonation, he and Ginevra had heard in that far-off bell tower of Votivkirche. Not only that, but the sterility was gone! The current which had been turned on inside him leaped to his hands and fingers.

At last he was ready.

Michael immediately discarded the fall concert repertoire, chosen as it had been merely for showmanship reasons, and substituted a new musical menu for the old. Ever so carefully, as a master chef prepares a banquet for royalty, he selected his individual items. In fact, he agonized over them, for each number must not only mesh with all the others, but enhance as well, gradually building into a crescendo which would trumpet a musical vision of his new life.

Much more complicated was the matter of his new

recording. How could he stop the process at such a late date? Not surprisingly, when he met with Polygram management and dropped his bombshell, they were furious. Only with much effort was he able to calm them down— and that on a premise they strongly doubted: that his replacement would be so much better that they would be more than compensated for double the expected production expense!

He walked out of their offices in a very subdued mood. If he had retained any illusions about how low his musical stock had sunk, that meeting would have graphically settled the question. If his new recording failed to sell well, he would almost certainly be dropped from the label.

Then, he memorized all the numbers before making his trial run recording; this way, he was able to give his undivided attention to interpretation before wrapping up the process. Only after he himself was thoroughly satisfied with the results did he have it recorded and then hand-carried by his agent to Deutsche Grammophon/Polygram management.

He didn't have to wait very long; only minutes after they played his pilot recording, Michael received a long-distance phone call from the president himself. Michael had known him for years and knew him to be a very tough *hombre* indeed. Recognizing full well that he and the company lived and died by the bottom line, he was used to making decisions for the most pragmatic of reasons. And recording artists feared him because he had a way of telling the unvarnished truth sans embellishments or grace notes. And now he was on the line. Initially almost speechless, he finally recovered and blurted out, "What has happened, Michael? For years now, your recordings have seemed—pardon my candidness, but you know blunt me—a bit tinny, fluffy, sometimes listless, and even a bit . . . uh . . . for want of a better word, 'peevish,' more or less as if you were irritably going through the motions again, but with little idea why. Now, here, on the other hand, comes a recording which sounded to us like you woke up one morning and decided to belatedly take control of your life and career; that there were new and exciting ways of interpreting music: interpreting with power . . . and beauty . . . and, I might add, Michael . . . a promise of depth and seasoning we quite frankly no longer believed was in you! *What has happened?*"

That incredible summer passed in a blur of activity. The long ebb over at last, the incoming tidal forces of Michael's life now thundered up the beaches of the musical world.

Deutsche Grammophon management and employees worked around the clock to process, release, and then market what they firmly believed would be the greatest recording of his career. Word leaked out even before it was released. Consequently, there was a run on it when it hit the market. All of this translated into enthusiastic interest in his fall concert schedule.

Early in August, before the recording had been released, Michael phoned his New York agent, who could hardly contain himself about the new bookings which were flooding in for the North American tour, spring of the following year. Michael, after first swearing him to secrecy, told him that he was entrusting to his care the most delicate assignment of their long association—one which, if botched, would result in irreparable damage. The agent promised to fulfill his instructions.

He wanted of him three things: to trace the whereabouts of a certain lady (taking great pains to ensure that the lady in question would not be aware of the search process); to find out if the lady had married; to process a mailing (the contents of the mailing would be adjusted according to whether the lady had married or not).

Meanwhile, Ginevra played the waiting game—a very hard game to play without great frustration. And, for her, the frustration level had been steadily building for almost three years. *When* would she know?

Within a year after mailing her first book, she felt reasonably confident that he was reading what she had sent. But she had little data upon which to base her assumptions. During the second year, little snips of information relating to possible change in Devereaux appeared here and there. Nothing really significant, really, but enough to give her hope.

She had knelt down by her bed that memorable morning before she mailed Thompson's poems. In her heartfelt supplication, she voiced her conviction that, with this book, she had now done all that was in her power to do. The rest was up to Him. Then she drove down the mountain to the Boulder Post Office and sent it to her New York relayer, and returned home to wait.

It was several months before the Devereaux-related excitement in the music world began to build. Her heart beat a lilting "allegro" the day she first heard about the growing interest in Michael's new recording. She could hardly wait to get a copy.

Then came the day when, in her mailbox, there appeared a little yellow piece of paper indicating that a registered piece of mail was waiting for her in the post office. It turned out to be a *very large* package from an unknown source in New York.

Not until she had returned to her chalet did she open it. Initially, she was almost certain that one of her former students was playing a joke on her, for the box was dispro- portionately light. She quickly discovered the reason: It was jammed full with wadded-up paper. Her room was half full of paper before she discovered the strange-shaped box at the very bottom of the mailing carton. . . . *What* could it be? . . . *Who* could it be from? . . . In this box, obviously packed with great care, were five items, each separated by a hard cardboard divider: a perfect flame-red rose in a sealed moisture-tight container, Michael's new Deutsche Grammophon recording, a publicity poster of a concert program which read as follows:

MICHAEL DEVEREAUX

FIRST CHRISTMAS EVE CONCERT

VIENNA OPERA HOUSE

(followed by the other data giving exact time and date), a round-trip airline ticket to Vienna, and, at the very bottom, in an exquisite gold box, a front section ticket to the concert.

Fearing someone in the Standing section would take her place before she could reach her seat, during the enthusiastic applause following Bach's "Italian Concerto," Ginevra asked an usher to escort her to her seat in the third row. Michael, who had turned to acknowledge the applause, caught the motion: the beautiful woman coming down the aisle. And she was wearing a flame-red rose. Even in Vienna, a city known for its beautiful women, she was a sight to pin dreams on.

How terribly grateful he was to the audience for continuing to clap, for that gave him time, precious time in which to restore his badly damaged equilibrium. It was passing strange, mused Michael. For years now, both his greatest dream and his greatest nightmare were one and the same: that Ginevra would actually show up for one of his concerts. The nightmare had to do with deep-seated fear that her presence in the audience would inevitably destroy his concentration, and with it the concert itself. And now, *here* she was! If he ever needed a higher power, he needed it now. Briefly, he bowed his head. When he raised it, he felt again this new sense of serenity, peace, and command.

Leaving the baroque world of Bach, he now turned to

César Franck; being a composer of romantic music, but with baroque connections, Michael had felt him to be a perfect bridge from Bach to Martin and Prokofiev. As he began to play Franck's "Prelude: Chorale et Fugue," he settled down to making this the greatest concert of his career. He had sometimes envied the great ones their announced conviction that, for each, the greatest concert was always the very next one on the schedule—they *never* took a free ride on their laurels. Only this season it had been that he had joined the masters, belatedly recognizing that the greatest thanks he could ever give his Maker would be to extend his powers to the limits, every time he performed, regardless of how large or how small the crowd.

The Opera House audience had quickly recognized the almost mind-boggling change in attitude. The last time he had played here, reviewers had unkindly but accurately declared him washed up. So desperate for success of any kind had he become that he openly pandered to what few people still came. It was really pathetic: He would edge out onto the platform like an abused puppy, cringing lest he be kicked again. Not surprisingly, what he apparently expected, he got.

Now there was never any question as to who was in control. On the second, he would stride purposefully onto the stage, with a pleasant look on his face, and gracefully bow. He would often change his attire between sections, adding a visual extra to the auditory. His attire was always impeccable: newly cleaned and pressed, and he was neither over- nor underdressed for the occasion.

But neither was he proud, recognizing just how fragile is the line between success and failure, and how terribly difficult it is to stay at the top once you get there. Nor did he anymore grovel or play to the galleries. The attitude he now projected was, quite simply: *I'm so pleased you honored me by coming out tonight. I have prepared long and hard for this occasion, consequently it is both my intent and my expectation that we shall share the greatest musical hour and a half of our lifetimes.*

Ginevra felt herself becoming part of a living, breathing island in time. Every concert performed well, is that: kind of a magic moment during which outside life temporarily ceases to be. Great music, after all, is outside of time and thus not subject to its rules. Thus it was that Ginevra, like the Viennese audience, lost all sense of identity, as Devereaux's playing became all the reality they were to know for some time.

These weren't just notes pried from a reluctant piano they were hearing; this was life itself, life with all its frustrations and complexities.

With such power and conviction did César Franck speak from the grave that the audience stood applauding

❖

for three minutes at the end of the first half. In fact, disregarding Opera House protocol, a number of the younger members of the audience swarmed onto the stage and surrounded Michael before he could get backstage. The new Michael stopped, and with a pleasant look on his face all the while, autographed every last program that was shoved at him. Nay, more than that: as one of these autograph seekers, jubilant of face, came back to Ginevra's row, she saw him proudly showing the program to his parents. Michael had taken the trouble to learn each person's name so he could inscribe each one personally!

Michael's tux was wringing wet. As for the gleaming black Boesendorfer, with such superhuman energy had Michael attacked it that it begged for the soothing balm of a piano tuner's ministrations; hence it was wheeled out for a badly needed rest. In its place was the monarch of the city's Steinway grands. Michael had specifically requested this living nine feet of history. No one knew for sure just how old it was, but it had for years been the pride and joy of Horowitz. Rubinstein would play here on no other, and it was even rumored that the great Paderewski performed on it. Michael, like all real artists, deeply loved his favorite instruments. Like the fabled Velveteen Rabbit, when an instrument such as this Steinway has brought so much happiness, fulfillment, meaning, and love into life . . . well, over the years, it ceases to be just a piano and approaches personhood. Thus it was that Michael, before it was wheeled in, had a heart-to-heart chat with it.

A stagehand, watching the scene, didn't even lift an eyebrow—concert musicians were *all* a loony bunch.

Only after a great deal of soul-searching had Michael decided to open the second half of his concert with Swiss-born Frank Martin's "Eight Preludes." He had long appreciated and loved Martin's fresh approach to music, his lyrical euphonies. Martin reminded Michael of the American composer Howard Hanson. He often had a difficult time choosing which one to include in a given repertoire; but this season, it was Martin's turn.

More and more sure of himself, Michael only gained in power as he retold Martin's story; by the time he finished the Preludes, he owned Vienna. The deafening applause rolled on and on. And nobody appeared willing to ever sit down.

Finally, the house quiet once again, a microphone was brought out and Michael stepped up to speak.

"Ladies and gentlemen," he began, "I have a substitution to make. As you know, I am scheduled to perform Prokofiev's 'Sonata #6 in A Major, Opus 82' as my concluding number, but I hope you will not be *too* disappointed"—and here he smiled his boyish grin—"if I substitute a piece which I composed, a piece which has never before been performed in public."

He paused, then continued: "Ten years ago tonight, in this fair city, this piece of music was born, but it was not completed until late this spring. I have been saving it for tonight." And here, he dared to glance in the direction of Ginevra.

"The title is 'Variations on a Theme by Massenet.' "

Nothing in Michael's composing experience had been more difficult than deciding what to do with "Meditation." And the difficulties did not fall away with his conversion. He still had some tough decisions to face: Should his variations consist merely as creative side trips from that one melodic base? By doing so, he knew he could dazzle. Should the variations be limited to musical proof that he and his Maker were now friends? With neither was he satisfied.

Of all the epiphanies he had ever experienced, none could compare with the one which was born to him one "God's in His Heaven/All's right with the world" spring morning. He realized that he could create a counterpart to what Massenet had done with the "Meditation" intermezzo: a fusion of earthly love with the divine. Belatedly, he recognized a great truth: God does not come to us in the abstract—He comes to us through flesh and blood. We do not initially fall in love with God as a principle; rather, we first fall in love with human beings whose lives radiate friendship with the divine. It is only *then* that we seek out God on our own.

Ginevra was such a prototype—that is why he had fallen in love with her. And he had little doubt in his mind but that it was she who had choreographed his conversion. No one else had he ever known who would have cared enough to institute and carry out such a flawless plan of action. Besides, some of the book choices made him mighty suspicious.

Michael had also recognized what all true artists do sooner or later: that their greatest work must come from within, from known experience. If he was to endow his variations with power akin to the original, they must emanate from the joys and sorrows that made him what he was, and since she and God were inextricably woven together in Michael's multihued bolt of life, then woven together they must remain throughout the composition.

It would not be acceptable for her to distance herself and pretend she could judge what he had become dispassionately. No, Ginevra must enter into the world he had composed . . . and decide at the other end whether or not she would stay.

In Ginevra's mind, everything seemed to harken back to that cold night in the tower of Votivkirche, for it was there that two lives, only hours from oneness, had seen the cable of their intertwining selves unravel in only seconds.

Furthermore, there was more than God holding them apart. More than her romanticism as compared to his realism. That far-off exchange of words had highlighted for her some significant problems which, left unresolved, would preclude marriage even if Michael *had* been converted. Let's see: How could she conceptualize them?

Essentially, it all came down to these. Michael had laughed at and ridiculed her deepest-felt feelings. Had made light of her tears. Had shown a complete absence of empathy. Worse yet, he exhibited a clear-cut absence of the one most crucial character trait in the universe: *Kindness.*

Also, at no time since she had known him had she ever seen him admit in any way that he was wrong about anything—and compounding the problem, he had refused to disclose his true identity to her:

There had been a locked door halfway down to his heart.

There had been another locked door halfway up to his soul.

As far as she knew, both doors were still closed.

But if they ever *were* to be unlocked, "Meditation" would be the key.

As-soft-as-a-mother's-touch pianissimo, Michael begins to play. So softly that there appear to be no breaks at all between the notes, but rather a continuous skein of melodic sound. And, for the first time in Michael's career, there is a flowing oneness with the piano: impossible to tell where flesh, blood, and breath end and where wood, ivory, and metal join.

Ginevra cannot help but feel tense in spite of blurred fingers weaving dreams around her. Deep down, she knows that what occurs during *this* piece of music will have a profound effect upon the rest of her life. And the rest of Michael's life.

But she didn't travel so many thousands of miles just to be a referee or a critic. If their two worlds are ever to be one, she must leave her safe seat in the audience and step into the world of Michael's composition. Strangely enough—and living proof that it is the "small" things in life which are often the most significant—Michael's exhibition of kindness to the young people who blocked his exit during intermission strongly predisposes her in his favor.

How beautifully his arpeggios flow, cascading as serenely as Alpine brooks singing their way down to the sea. All nature appears to be at peace. As Michael plays, she can envision the birds' wake-up calls, the falling rain and drifting snow, the sighing of her dear pines, and the endless journey of the stars. The world is a beautiful place . . . and love is in the air.

Suddenly, she stiffens. Certainly those are bells she is hearing. Yes, Christmas bells, flooding the universe with joy. She listens intently as their pealing grows ever louder—then *that theme!* It begins to mesh with the bells, but only for an instant. Right in the middle of it, there is an ominous shift from major to minor key, and from harmony to dissonance. And the bells! In that selfsame instant, the pealing joy ceases and is replaced by tolling sorrow. How uncannily perfect is Michael's capture of that moment when all the joy in their world went sour.

The dissonance and tolling eventually give way to a classical music potpourri. Here and there she recognizes snatches of well-known themes, some of them from piano concertos. But the notes are clipped off short and played perfunctorily: more or less as if the pianist doesn't much care how they sound as long as they all get played in record time. Several times, the Theme tries to edge in, but each time it is rudely repulsed.

Now it is that Dvorak's "New World Symphony" thunders in. Aha! At last, some resolution! Some affirmation! Not so. It quickly becomes apparent that this paean to a brave new world is, ironically, in steady retreat instead of advancing to triumph. Almost—it seems to her—as if it were a retrograde "Bolero": its theme progressively diminishing in power instead of increasing. Once again, "Meditation" seeks entry; once again, it is unceremoniously disposed of.

By now, Ginevra is deciphering Michael's musical code quite well. Vividly revealed has been the progressive deterioration of Michael both as a person and as a pianist:

From the moment in the cathedral tower when the bells began to toll, every variation that followed has dealt with the stages of his fall.

Then, clouds close in, thunder rumbles in the east, lightning strikes short-circuit the sky, and the rain falls. Torrents of it. Darkness sweeps in, and with it all the hells loose on this turbulent planet. Ginevra shivers as Michael stays in minor keys, mourning all the sadness and pain in the universe.

The winds gradually increase to hurricane strength. Far ahead of her—for she is exposed to the elements, too—she sees Michael, almost out of sight in the gloom, retreating from the storm. She follows, and attempts to call to him, but to no avail: The tempest swallows the words before they can be formed. Then the black clouds close in, and she loses sight of him altogether.

As the hurricane reaches ultimate strength, major keys are in full flight from the minors (Ginevra had discovered some time back that Michael is equating majors with the forces of Light, and minors with the forces of Darkness). It does not seem possible that any force on earth could save Michael from destruction.

It is now in the darkest midnight, when the few majors left are making their last stand. She senses that, for Michael, the end is near. Now, when she has all but conceded victory to the Dark Power, she again hears the strains of Thais's Theme! How can such a frail thing possibly survive when leagued against the legions of Darkness? But, almost unbelievably, it does.

At this instant, Ginevra chances to look with wide-open eyes at not Michael the pianist, but Michael the man. He has clearly forgotten all about the world, the concert audience, even *her*. In his total identification with the struggle for his soul, he is playing for only two beings: himself—the penitent sinner—and God. And his face? Well, never afterward could she really explain, but one thing was absolutely certain: there before her was Michael's naked soul.

With Michael's surrender, the tide turns at last: The storm rages on, but the enemy is now unmistakably in retreat. Dissonance and minors contest every step of the battlefield, trying vainly to hold off the invading Light. Then victorious majors begin sweeping the field.

Ginevra discovers in all this a great truth: It is minors that reveal the full beauty of majors. Had she not heard "Meditation" sobbing on the ropes of a minor key, she would never have realized the limitless power of God. It is the minor key that gives texture and beauty to the major; and it is dissonance that, by contrast, reveals the glory of harmony. It is sorrow that brings our wandering feet back to God.

❖

Finally, with the mists beginning to dissipate and the sun to break through, the Theme reappears, but alone for the first time. Now it is that Ginevra feels the full upward pull of the music, for "Meditation" soars Heavenward with such passion, pathos, and power that gravity is powerless to restrain it.

And Ginevra . . . her choice made . . . reaches up,
and with Michael,
climbs the stairs of heaven to God.

DEDICATION

This story is dedicated to my dearly beloved brother Romayne, who himself is a living embodiment of all that is finest in the concert piano profession, and who lived in—and loved—Vienna for almost a third of a century. As for Votivkirche (depicted on page 190), not too long ago our daughter Michelle climbed this selfsame bell tower with her Uncle Romayne, who was, at that time, still performing in the cathedral every summer.

HOW THIS STORY CAME TO BE

For as far back as I can remember, I have been haunted by "Meditation"—every time I hear it, I cry. It has moved me as has no other piece of music in my lifetime. It was while listening to Zamfir's pan flute rendition of it that the dream for this story was born.

For a long time, I have wanted to articulate in story form a music-related narrative much like this, but until now lacked the vehicle, the glue which would hold the story together. All this Massenet's "Meditation" provided.

After having sketched out the story line, I let it germinate for several months. Up till that time, I knew nothing of "Meditation's" origins except its authorship. It was at this juncture that I brought in Ingrid Vargas, of Takoma Park, Maryland—herself a pianist and organist—and one of my dear soul sisters. I sketched out the story line to her and asked if she would collaborate with me. She agreed to do some research on the work's origins. I'll admit I was mighty apprehensive: What if the piece proved—as was more than likely—to have no religious tie-ins at all; worse yet: had its roots in the opposite camp?

I'll never forget the day Ms. Vargas came bursting into my office, in great excitement exclaiming, "Dr. Wheeler, you were right!" Upon getting her calmed down, she showed me the results of her research: that the piece was composed as a bridge between the secular and spiritual realms of our lives. Additionally, Ms. Vargas helped

❖